The Ministry of Motherhood

CHERYL LACEY DONOVAN

Copyright © 2009 by Cheryl Lacey Donovan

ISBN-10: 0-9790222-3-1
ISBN-13: 978-0-9790222-3-4
Library of Congress Control Number: 2008938897

Publisher's Note
Printed and bound in the United States of America. All rights reserved. No part of this book may be reproduced or transmitted in any form or by any means, electronic or mechanical, including photocopying, recording, or by an information storage and retrieval system-except by a reviewer who may quote brief passages in a review to be printed in a magazine, newspaper, or on the Web-without permission in writing from the publisher.

Although the author and publisher have made every effort to ensure the accuracy and completeness of information contained in this book, we assume no responsibility for errors, inaccuracies, omissions, or any inconsistency herein.

Scripture taken from the HOLY BIBLE, NEWINTERNATIONAL VERSION®. Copyright © 1973, 1978, 1984 International Bible Society. Used by permission of Zondervan. All rights reserved.

Scripture taken from the New King James Version.
Copyright © 1982 by Thomas Nelson, Inc. Used by permission. All rights reserved.

Scripture taken from the HOLY BIBLE, NEW INTERNATIONAL VERSION. Copyright © 1973, 1978, 1984 International Bible Society. Used by permission of Zondervan. All rights reserved.

Scripture quotations are taken from the Holy Bible, New Living Translation, copyright 1996, 2004. Used by permission of Tyndale House Publishers, Inc., Wheaton, Illinois 60189. All rights reserved.

Peace In The Storm Publishing, LLC.
P.O. Box 1152
Pocono Summit, PA 18346

Visit our Web site at www.PeaceInTheStormPublishing.com

"The twentieth of June 1966 was the happiest day of my life. This bundle of joy was my daughter. She was bright and alert. We played together and she learned very fast. I never had any problems with her.

Cheryl has been the joy of my life all of her life. I am very proud of her in everything she sets her mind to.

I will always love her with all of my heart. I could write forever and never be able to put in words what she means to me. "

Love,

Mom

Praise for

The Ministry of Motherhood

"Cheryl Lacey Donovan challenges women of all races, creeds, colors and circumstances to rise above their own conditions, to embrace and confront their realities, be stronger, wiser and better women and mothers while inspiring us all to fulfill the blessing of motherhood with dignity, respect and gratitude."
~Elissa Gabrielle, President & CEO
Peace In The Storm Publishing

"This book is like no other in it's genre. Many have attempted to tell the in and outs of motherhood but Cheryl Lacey Donovan administers it straight without the added puffers that's found in most books. The Ministry of Motherhood speaks to women on every level whether single, divorced, married or mothering those close to you, by embracing those Biblical principles that hold us all accountable to answering our call with due diligence."
~ Cherilyn Azubuike, author of *Weekly Wisdom: 52 Ways to Live a More Fulfilled Life*

"Like a master practitioner, Cheryl Donovan speaks poignant truth about the ministry of motherhood in a way that no only convicts the reader, but offers real solutions and hope with the challenges of the task. Her uncomplicated, literary writing style will appeal to readers from all age ranges and educational levels. Well done and definitely needed."
~Rhonda McKnight, author of *Secrets and Lies*

"All women face daily challenges ranging from abuse, poverty, racism, addictions and parent-teen problems, just to name a few. These challenges play the Devils advocate in many of our lives, causing so much emotional confusion. This book will help you, the reader, to be more aware of your enemy."
~*Womensselfesteem.com*

"Women face challenges everyday where trials and tribulations are added to the greater part of the whole spectrum of parenting...Cheryl Lacey Donovan's *The Ministry of Motherhood* shares one woman's story of triumph amid lessons learned from it. Read her inspiring story and what it takes to be a better mother."
~Alvin C. Romer, *The Romer Review*

The Ministry of Motherhood

CHERYL LACEY DONOVAN

Peace In The Storm Publishing, LLC

"I realized that everything concerning them depended on the sermon that my life would preach. Each scripture would be written by the words I spoke, the experiences I encountered, and the circumstances I overcame. As each chapter unfolded, I was determined it would have a happy ending. Their births were the Genesis, and, if Revelation was to end triumphantly, I needed to be their savior here on Earth."

~CHERYL LACEY DONOVAN

Acknowledgements

To God be the glory for the things He has done. Everything I am I owe to my Creator who is the author and finisher of my faith.

Because of Him, I was blessed with a mother whose unconditional love has sustained me.

Because of Him, my children are not statistics, but instead are blessed and highly favored.

Because of Him, I have found my Boaz Keith.

Because of Him, I have aligned myself with other single mothers; Francine, Alayniah, and Ashley, who are walking in there ministries as mothers.

Because of Him, I have crossed paths with the likes of Elissa Gabrielle, my publisher and Alvin C. Romer of *The Romer Review*.

Because of Him, I am an over comer by the words of this testimony, my testimony to an ever present God whose mercy and grace still sustain me.

Because of Him, through my testimony of His love others will see His glory and be saved.

Because of Him, I am.

INTRODUCTION

Mother is a verb. It's something you do, not just who you are. I learned the hard way. Who would have imagined it would happen to me -- a mother at sixteen! Why didn't I listen? Why had I engaged in premarital sex? These questions have reverberated in my mind many times over the years. I was smart enough to know the potential outcome. But, I did it anyway. It just felt so right. How did Tina Turner put it -- what's love got to do with it? Let me answer that for you. Nothing when your emotions collide with immaturity and stupidity. What a disastrous mix, to say the least. Dwelling on the obvious became a lesson in futility for me each time I looked into my children's eyes. I understood the monumental task that stood before me as I tried to make ends meet as a single mother. I lived and learned as God prepared me for a manifested destiny. It's called motherhood with a mission...a ministry. Every word I spoke, every move I made, affected two other innocent souls who didn't ask to be here. Without a choice, I had to pull myself together and prepare a sermon based on my life. I had to formulate meaningful text, outline life's lessons, and deliver the message loud and clear so that my children and others could be saved with God using me as a vessel.

I had every reason not to be a good mother. All the cards were stacked against me. Life's hurdles stood tall at every turn. I was a teenager and the victim of an abusive marriage. From being unable to get public assistance to my ex-husband refusing to pay child support, I was placed behind the eight ball every time. But, to be a mother is one of the most important tasks God has entrusted to women. God chose women as the vessels through which He would bring into being His most valuable creation: mankind.

Mothers are assigned with the task of developing, encouraging, nurturing, and cultivating the lives that are placed in their care. Our most important role is to teach our children about God, His principles, and His plans for their lives. True mothers don't throw in the towel when the going gets tough. Instead, they look for avenues that lead to destinations that can enhance their lives as well as the lives of their children. Mothers are charged with loving their children unconditionally. The bond that exists between a mother and child is a

The Ministry of Motherhood

special one. Faithful and dedicated mothers are the ones that are not afraid to dig down deep into the dirt and pull their children up from sure destruction. This type of love can only be compared to the Love of God for His children. Children are a blessed heritage from God. Mothers should always remember the value that God has placed on children. When He told His disciples, 'suffer the little children to come unto Me for such is the kingdom of heaven', He made it clear that children are important to Him. Mothers should view their role with importance.

This is my journey on the path we call motherhood; the ups, the downs, the good, the bad, and the ugly. I'd like to share with you my labor of love and dedication to make sure that others don't follow my path. Initially, I will share with you my angst upon finding out I was pregnant. Telling my mother was the hardest thing I've ever done. In Chapter three, you will discover the parallels between modern day single mothers and those in the Bible.

As the book progresses, the latter chapters deal with my adaptation to motherhood and the implied tenets of ministry-- chapters with such meaningful titles as Open Door Policy; The Abyss; Mama's Sermon; Innocence Lost; Happily Ever After; and The Cycle Begins, et al. Each one of these episodes give you a look inside my heart, my soul, my very being...sharing and digging deeper in myself for those nuggets of wisdom. I use biblical scriptures and 'thus sayeth the Lord' dictates to guide me. It's the ministry fundamentality that propels the outreach gesture so that you may be mindful of doing the right thing. This is what this book is all about.

The Discovery...

PROLOGUE

My sixteenth birthday had come and gone and what a birthday it was. It was the night I lost my virginity to the love of my life.

It began like any other night, replete with all the niceties that make for a wonderful experience—flowers, moonlight, and a warm summer breeze that gently caressed my face. It wasn't my intention, but intention gave way to desire as I felt myself falling deeper and deeper under the spell that would soon consume me.

"You say you love me, why don't you prove it. You shouldn't be so hard to get, girls sleep with me all the time but I don't love them, I love you. You know I wanna marry you. I don't understand why you won't just show me you love me."

His desire made me feel seductive, womanly. But his desires were born out of a control and conquer mentality that would later prove to be my demise. You see, his only intent was to prove that he could break me down, reel me in, and conquer my spirit.

"I do love him. He did promise to marry me. Surely it won't hurt this one time. But, what would my parents think? How could I betray them this way? But, if I don't do this I'll lose him forever. But, if he loved me wouldn't he wait?"

Conflicting thoughts and emotions filled my cup until it overflowed. Tasting from the forbidden fruit of sex was sweeter than anything I had ever known. Despite the voices in my head to the contrary, I wanted to indulge in the realm of the illicit; a walk on the wild side. Something I'd never done before, temptation.

Before long, common sense gave way to pure desire and I found myself indulging in acts too mature for my tender years.

When I got home, I suddenly found my conscience and began to feel the weight of what I had done. Rushing to the bathroom, I turned on the water and began scrubbing profusely to wash away the guilt and the shame of my indiscretion.

A few weeks later, my mother informed me she had made an appointment with the gynecologist for a checkup; "A well woman's exam, what is that?" I pondered. "Oh yeah, I remember talking about that in health class," I reasoned. "But, why does she want me to go

The Ministry of Motherhood

now? Could she know what I've done? No, that's impossible. Surely she can't just look at me and know. Would the doctor be able to tell what I had done?"

Little did I know at the time, finding out about my sexual imprudence was only the tip of the iceberg.

A PRAYER OF DECLARATION

I confess the will of God in the lives of the women and men that will read this book. Lord, I boldly call forth Your will to be done in their lives here on earth as it is in heaven. I cast out all of the assignments that the devil has sent against them, and I bind them here on earth so that they may be bound in heaven. I release all of the plans that You have for their lives, plans of good and not of evil, to give them a future and a hope, and I confess that those plans will be loosed in heaven so that they can be manifest here on earth. I declare that everyone that reads this book will be transformed into a new creature. As a result, I am expecting that they will receive favor and high esteem with You and with people.

Lord, I pray that priorities will be set in perfect order. Be Lord and Ruler over their hearts. Help them to find time to be alone with You. Lord, I confess that they will make Your word, prayer, and praise a priority in their lives. I confess that all who read this book will be the head and not the tail, they will be above and not beneath, they will be more than conquerors through Jesus Christ, and they will do all things through Christ who strengthens them. I decree and declare that generational curses of poverty, low self esteem, welfare use, and lack of education, lack of self control, stealing, cheating, dishonesty, rebellion, and deception will be broken, strongholds will be torn down, and breakthroughs will happen.

I declare that the captives will be set free to speak to the situations in their lives and that those situations will be changed. Position them to receive from You, God. Change old patterns and mindsets and replace them with thoughts of You and of Your word. Help them to remain steadfast as they seek to change their lives.

Help them to forgive themselves for the choices that they've made and the circumstances that they've allowed to occur. Help them to forgive others.

Lead them not into temptation, but deliver them from the evil one.

Now, unto the one who is able to present us faultless before the throne of grace, be all glory and honor, and majesty forever and ever. Amen.

CHAPTER ONE

"The Rabbit Died"

Exodus 20:12 Honor thy mother and thy father that thy days may be long upon the earth

I have never enjoyed going to the doctor. The atmosphere is always so cold and sterile. The floor in this particular exam room sparkled so brightly, that the glare from the fluorescent lights reminded me of sunlight bouncing off of the Gulf of Mexico in late summer. The containers that held the medical instruments were so shiny, that when you looked into them, you could see your reflection. The white walls appeared as if they had been recently painted, and each one had a poster of a different health care message that proclaimed the benefits of one drug or another.

I was undressed from the waist down. My feet were in the stirrups and my legs were about as far apart as they could go. It's a funny thing, but in the heat of passion, I don't ever remember feeling quite as embarrassed as I did in the doctor's office that day.

Although I had become sexually active, I was still not comfortable with my own body. Truth be told, in many ways I was very much an old fashioned girl. I didn't really like to be naked in front of anyone else. The thought of a stranger probing around my private parts filled me with an embarrassment that could only be described as demoralizing.

This was not exactly my idea of fun. It was my first well woman's exam, and if it was left up to me, it would surely be my last.

Thoughts ran uncontrollably through my head. Each of my one hundred billion brain cells must've been at work that day.

"Had I remembered to wash properly? Will the doctor be able to tell that I had been sexually active? Would he tell my mother?"

I would soon find out that telling my mother about my sexual encounter would be the least of my worries.

The doctor's bedside manners left a lot to be desired. He hardly looked at me. He said even fewer words. The fluorescent lights bounced off his bald head. The brightness blinded me as he methodically and mechanically did his business between my legs. He asked the nurse to pass

The Ministry of Motherhood

him his instruments. I could see him peering over his bifocals as if he disapproved of her delivery. The instruments that he used were cold and hard. Uncomfortable and embarrassed, it felt like the doctor was stretching me into all kinds of unusual positions. I could only imagine that my private parts would soon snap back at him like a rubber band and trap him in the abyss.

As he inserted the instrument for the first time, he pinched the side of my vagina and a pain that I can't explain quickly made its way up my spine. All I prayed for was that the invasion would soon be over.

After the examination, the doctor quickly left the room. His haste made me uneasy.

"Why had the doctor left so abruptly? What was taking him so long to return?" I questioned. Thirty minutes seemed like an eternity as I sat waiting. Finally, the door slowly opened and I could see the doctor's beet red face. His deep wrinkles signaled to me that he was disturbed by something. The doctor looked over his bifocals once more. This time, his disdain was obviously directed toward me. It was the kind of look that your parents give you when you've done something wrong.

The doctor finally spoke, but what I heard came out of his mouth in slow motion. What he had to say left me limp and lifeless. The room began to spin. His revelation made me feel faint and dizzy.

"You must be mistaken," I said.

He began with all the sternness of an angry father speaking to his rebellious teen. "Have you been sexually active?"

I could feel my face burning with contempt at the question. How dare he ask me something so personal. I looked down at the floor as if the answer to the doctor's question was going to jump up and hit me in the face.

"Yes," I said indignantly as I followed up with, "but I haven't missed a period." I believed this piece of information would somehow nullify the doctor's findings.

"That doesn't mean anything," he said smugly as he glared over his bifocals once more.

My face, once again, became flushed as it burned like a flame from hell's fire. The shame and embarrassment that I felt at the thought of what I had done was more than I could bear. Feeling like I had just been hit with a ton of bricks, I wanted to slip away into oblivion, never to be seen again.

"God, just take me now," I remember whispering.

Secretly, I knew that being taken away would be the easy way out. Funny, but at that moment, being somewhere else seemed easier than having to tell my parents that their sixteen year old daughter was pregnant.

For a brief moment, I drifted away into my own thoughts. I was quickly brought back to reality by the doctor's next question.

"Shall I call your mother in to tell her the news or will you tell her yourself?" the doctor asked.

The Ministry of Motherhood

What kind of question was that? Surely he knew that I wasn't prepared to drop this bombshell on my mother right now. What would I say? How would I say it? Is he crazy? Tell her in front of all these people so they can see the disappointment and embarrassment on her face; hear it in her voice? The anxiety of the moment immediately set in. My mouth became dry, my hands were moist, and my heart was pounding.

"No," I answered quickly, almost in a whisper. The volume of my voice weakened by the heaviness of the news, the earth-shattering reality which was planted into my lap.

My stomach became queasy as the butterflies jumped about like a fish out of water. My entire body began to shake chaotically; the racing of my heart set panic into my entire being.

"I'll tell her myself later," I revealed, still unsure if I would.

"Very well then, but you have to do it soon because we need to set up your prenatal visit as soon as possible."

"Thank you," I said tearfully.

That night seemed to last forever. I agonized over the decision I had to make. I feared revealing to my mother the truth about my condition. The thought of what would occur played over and over in my mind. I imagined the scenario repeatedly, and with each vision, I became more scared, more nervous, and tearfully alarmed. Each tick of the clock became louder and louder, like the beat of a messenger drum in the distance. The night drew on. I thought it would never end.

My thoughts were filled with the dreams and desires that my mother and I had discussed for as long as I could remember. She had been the most influential part of my life: shaping me, molding me, and teaching me how to become a strong, independent young woman. Now look at the mess I'd made. How on earth could I be independent when I now had a dependent? How would I raise a child?

CHAPTER TWO

"News Flash"

Proverbs 1:8-9 Listen my son to your father's instruction and do not forsake your mother's teaching. They will be a garland to grace your head and a chain to adorn your neck.

Waiting to break the news to my mother was my choice, but it probably would have been better to allow the doctor to help me, especially since I waited nearly two more weeks to tell her. Even then, the doctor beat me to it because he had already called my unexpecting mother to set up a prenatal visit with me later that week. I suppose like any other teenager, I believed that somehow this problem would miraculously work itself out without my having to face the music. I guess I believed that if I prayed hard enough, everything would go away.

When my mother called me into her room, I could tell in her voice that something was wrong. I had no idea that she had spoken to the doctor earlier that day.

"Is there anything you want to tell me?" she questioned.

Immediately, I began to feel butterflies in my stomach. Tension had mounted throughout my body and I wanted to rush to the bathroom to relieve myself, but I was afraid to move. I sensed what was going on and the water works began. Crying profusely, I didn't know what kind of response I would get. The only reference I had was when one of my aunts tried to literally beat the baby out of my cousin. My mother had never been one for physical violence against her children, but this was different. I didn't know how she'd respond. I had always been so desperate for her approval, and now, I was sure she would be devastated. The anticipation was unbearable. The apprehension, the tension was so thick, you could cut it with a knife. Even so, all I wanted to know was that my mother still loved me and would be there for me just as she had always been. It's funny; no matter how old you are, or what type of triumph or tragedy you experience, there's nothing in this world that compares to the comfort of a mother. I so desperately needed that comfort from her; I needed to know that she loved me, in spite of myself, and despite my circumstance.

The Ministry of Motherhood

My fears soon subsided as we both found ourselves in a loving embrace that was tempered with tears which flowed like rivers of running water. This was a true example of the ministry of motherhood. My mother was never afraid to face the tough challenges. She never shyed away from helping her children rise like a phoenix from the ashes of their lives.

A potpourri of emotions consumed me whole at that point. My feelings were all running together; relief, sadness, fear, and pain, all at the same time. Ironically, I felt a sense of joy at the thought of bringing a life into this world. I was blessed, in that my mother birthed me.

Faced with conflicting sentiments was somewhat confusing, and left me with a sense of guilt. Joy and pain challenged my feelings. On one hand, I knew with all of my heart that I hurt my mother; yet, I was going to be a mother. How could that be all bad? How could something so tremendous be so terrifying?

MARY

*Luke 1:28 Gabriel appeared to her and said,
"Greetings, favored woman!
The Lord is with you."*

Mary was a quiet girl and she kept to herself. Her life was not very interesting. She was a virgin from a poor family. She studied, worked hard, and spent time with the other girls her age. Mary was considered lucky because she had already met someone, and he was the most handsome man in town. He was from a good family and people liked him. Mary's parents were very happy with her choice.

Mary had really never given anyone a moment's concern, until the day Gabriel appeared to her. She must've been scared because she cowered in fear when the angel appeared. Yet, part of her was secretly delighted about the news she received because she immediately said yes to God's plan for her life. She was going to have a baby.

Under ordinary circumstances, this news would be cause for celebration. But, she wasn't married, and she was only fifteen. She knew she had to face Joseph and she was prepared for the worst. They had planned to get married and he had big dreams for their future. Now everything would be different because of this baby; a baby that was not his.

Joseph was shocked and hurt by the news. He demanded to know the name of the baby's father. When Mary told him, he didn't believe her. He believed Mary had cheated on him.
In spite of it all, Joseph still loved Mary.
Mary gave birth to her first son in poverty. No midwives were there to help her and she didn't have a comfortable bed. It was cold and she was a stranger in a strange city.

Joseph married Mary, and together, they brought a new life into the world and raised him. They moved many times, for many reasons. It was difficult to live without any other family around to help. Their lives were never easy.

Her son looked like other children, but Mary knew that he was unique, and she knew why. Joseph loved the boy, but Mary knew that he could never forget the child was not his own.

Mary was an unwed, teen-aged mother. Her life entailed great personal sacrifice. She must've endured times of confusion, fear, and loneliness as the events of her life unfolded. She

The Ministry of Motherhood

survived the trials of a difficult life and the emotional pain through faith. She knew with certainty that God would sustain her.

Today, many mothers experience the same societal responses. They find themselves in a cycle of poverty that is often difficult to break. Knowing and believing that God, the Father, recognizes the important role a mother plays in her children's lives should be a comfort when mothers are experiencing times of confusion and fear.

Confusion and fear were my new best friends. The constant care required by my new son drained me. I no longer had a life of my own. Everything I did revolved around him. A relaxing bath, a good night's sleep; my most basic needs were put on hold indefinitely. Sometimes getting up in the morning was the hardest thing I had to do. When was the mother's instinct going to kick in? I was a girl trying to do a woman's job.

When my son was sick, ambivalent feelings crowded my mind. One moment, I felt compassion for my child, and the next minute I felt burdened by his demands. Powerless and frustrated beyond words, I'd find myself sobbing uncontrollably at my failure to make it all better.

Praying to God was my answer and He would always temper my racing thoughts with His love. Finally kicking in, my motherly instincts were not always enough and I would find myself praying to God for the wisdom to continue.

Being a mother can be both the best and the worst job all rolled into one. It can bring you immense joy and unbearable pain. At times, you will feel successful. At other times, you feel like a complete failure.

The good news is God's thoughts for you are thoughts of good and not of evil, to give you a future and a hope. If God allows a child to be born into this world, He is more than capable of giving you the strength and the resources to care for your child. Seek God for wisdom and knowledge. He is faithful and He will provide what you need.

As a mother, it is important that you develop a prayer life. A personal relationship with God will allow you to call forth those plans that God has for you. Ask God to make you a mother like Mary. Ushering in God's plans for your children's lives by expressing God's character, His power, His forgiveness, and His grace, will bring you honor. Your children will rise up and call you blessed. Knowing that God has taken control will give you peace once you have given your children back to Him, and partnered with Him as you pray for every aspect of their lives.

A PRAYER FOR CHILDREN

Lamentations 2:19 Pour out your hearts like water to the Lord. Lift up your hands to him in prayer, pleading for your children.

God, Your word says that children are a heritage from You. Teach us to train our children up in the way that they should go so that when they are old they will not depart from it. Remind us of the value that you placed on children when You told the disciples to suffer the little children to come unto me for such is the kingdom of heaven.

I confess that mothers will place their children in greater prominence in their hearts than careers, friends, or activities. Lord, bless our children and cause Your favor, love, and joy to be upon them.

Help us as parents to be good examples for our children, just as Christ was an example for us. Help us to exhibit the same type of parenting style with our children that You, our Father, demonstrate with us Your children. Give us the ability to love unconditionally, to be patience, to be kind. Teach us how to balance the hand of discipline with the hand of training and mercy.

Forgive us as parents, God, for not being good examples before our children. Forgive us for not being patient and kind toward them, forgive us for not exhibiting self control during moments of discipline. Help us to forgive our children for being disobedient.

Lead us not into temptation, but deliver us from the evil one.

Now unto the King eternal, immortal, invisible, the only wise God, we give You praise and glory forever, Amen.

CHAPTER THREE

"Cry Me a River"

Psalms 34:4 I sought the Lord and He heard me He delivered me from all my fears.

Alone in my room and out of the sight of my parents, tears would rush down my face like Niagara Falls. I'd cry for hours on end wondering if I would ever be able to make this up to my family. Night after night, my pillow would be soaked with tears. My pain flooded into a waterfall of emotions. Evidence of my misery and sadness was displayed the next day; one could barely see the whites of my eyes because of the redness and swelling.

All kinds of thoughts would crowd my mind. One concern that grew more prevalent by the day was the reality of the fact that my mother was in her second marriage. I felt very guilty about placing an additional burden on my step father, who surely had not bargained for taking care of another child.

Scared, uncertain and anxious, all of these emotions welled up inside me like a fist balled up in the middle of my stomach. I can remember looking at myself in the mirror regularly as I watched my stomach grow into a basketball sized monstrosity. I remember priding myself in the fact that my belly button was an "inny" and not an "outy." Silly what girls think about. Nevertheless, that was no longer the case.

They say the truth is allowed in Heaven. Yet, the truth of my existence was harsh and my reality began to set in. My hopes and dreams were fading fast. My life was flashing right before my eyes. It was common knowledge that teen mothers had to go on welfare and live in the projects with their sorry excuses for men who, more often than not, were duckin' and dodgin' the welfare workers so that the mother could keep her benefits. Everyone knew that teenage mothers never amounted to anything.

How would I continue my education now? Teen moms *never* finish school nor do their offspring. They were doomed to public assistance and substandard housing. Their choices were limited and their only hope was to acquire a minimum wage job at a fast food restaurant; or so they say.

The plan for me had always been to graduate from high school, attend college, and get a good,

The Ministry of Motherhood

high paying job. How was this going to happen now? Last but not least, what of my father, the pastor? How would he live this one down? How would he and our family withstand the ridicule that was sure to come our way from the good ole' church goin' folk? There's no way they would overlook this. After all, we had an image to uphold. How would that look? The pastor's daughter fornicating and all. 'He can't even control his own daughter, how can he tell us what to do?' I could hear it all loud and clear.

Being in a ministerial family wasn't easy. My father spent all of his time building an image that likened him to God. He was obligated to the church. He took that obligation very seriously. From his pristine looks to his austere demeanor, everything about him demanded respect from the religious community.

He traveled the busy highways each weekend to officiate each church service. He visited members who were in the hospital and he presided over funerals and weddings. Outward appearances would indicate a home life that was perfect. Realistically, our family was no different from any other; full of problems. My mother and father divorced when I was four. That alone sent shock waves through the church community. Nonetheless, we were still to maintain the image of a picture perfect family; him in his place and my mother and I in ours.

On special church occasions, my Dad bought me new clothes and I was allowed to travel with him. I endured the fake smiles and the meaningless conversation all in hopes of winning his approval. It didn't matter to me that I was a token as long as I got a chance to spend time with Daddy. So, you see how being pregnant at 16 was against all the rules of engagement. The facade of perfection would be shattered and everyone would know that we were real people.

This was going to be a tough road, but there was one thing I knew for sure. I wouldn't have to walk it alone.

THE MINISTRY OF MOTHERHOOD

1Kings 17:24 Then the woman said to Elijah, Now I know that you are a man of God and that the word of the Lord from your mouth is the truth.

If we are honest, we all must acknowledge that the circumstances we find ourselves in are a direct reflection of the choices we make; good or bad.

The first lesson you learn as a minister of motherhood is "Mama's baby, Daddy's maybe." You see, we know beyond a shadow of a doubt that when we give birth, our babies belong to us. If we are not ready for the sacrifices that come along with being a mother, then we should take whatever precautions necessary to prevent the resulting consequences of lying down with a man.

Our children don't get to choose how they begin their lives. Therefore, it's our responsibility to make sure that they have the best foundation possible.

For we wrestle not against flesh and blood, but against **principalities**, *against* **powers**, *against the rulers of the darkness of this world, against spiritual wickedness in high places. Ephesians 6:12)* Fighting a war that is spiritual at its roots, but very real and practical as it impacts our children, leaves us at a disadvantage if we don't equip ourselves with the proper battle gear. The spoils of this war are the souls of our children.

God desires that our children know they are fearfully and wonderfully made, created to do good works in Jesus Christ. The world, on the other hand, desires to strip them of their self worth, even their very lives.

Winning the war at all costs is Satan's desire. Playing neither fair nor playing to lose the enemy's battle, plans are already drawn and the self worth, character, and values of our children are at stake. Conquering Satan can only be done through our faith in God, and by living God's word and teaching it to our children through our examples This is the only way we can expect to win the war.

God has entrusted us as mothers with the awesome task of nurturing, teaching, and encouraging our children. They are God's assignment for us.

The Ministry of Motherhood

Excusing ourselves from this assignment by saying the father isn't around is not an option. The only option God affords us as a mother is to take care of our children. Accountability and fearlessness in taking the steps necessary to provide the quality of life our children deserve is God's expectation.

Nowhere else is the true meaning of motherhood more profoundly demonstrated than in the story told in I Kings 3.

This story speaks of two women who had given birth.

One of the women accidentally smothered her baby while sleeping. She then tried to claim the other woman's child as her own.

Solomon, the king at the time, decided that the only way to handle the situation was to divide the child into two equal parts. He would then give each woman a piece of the child.

The real mother of the child cried out to Solomon to give her child to the other mother whole, rather than divide him into two pieces.

The other woman declared that if she could not have the child, the real mother could not have him either. She admonished Solomon to continue.

Solomon, having prayed to God for wisdom, discerned that the woman who had exhibited the most love, compassion, and concern for the child's well being had to be his true mother.

From the time a child is carried in your womb, to the dreams deferred personal sacrifice is a primary principle of this ministry.

Somehow though, we've gotten the idea that all we need to do as mothers is to get our children up in the morning, feed them (maybe), dress them (maybe), and get them to school. We have all but handed over to the school system the responsibility of teaching our children. This is not only unacceptable, it is unbiblical.

The Bible tells us the family is the basic source for moral and practical teaching.

"These commandments that I give you today are to be upon your hearts. Impress them on your children. Talk about them when you sit at home and when you walk along the road, when you lie down and when you get up. (Deut 6:6-7).

It also tells us women are a vital link in that teaching. Taking back the responsibility of raising our children is the only remedy for the social ills that plague our society..

You'll hear people say children don't come with instructions. Not true. God has inspired the greatest manual of all, the Bible. In it are instructions for every aspect of life.

We mistakenly believe the trials we go through are new or are limited to our time, so we neglect to consult the greatest "How To" manual of all time... There's nothing new under the sun.

Slavery, abuse, murder, homosexuality, prostitution, corrupt governments, all of these things were around during biblical times. Confusion over gender roles, marital relationships, and a growing sense of hopelessness can all be found in the nation of Israel. Political alliances were torn apart, entire

The Ministry of Motherhood

villages were destroyed by violence, and female victimization was everywhere. Does this sound at all familiar?

Yet, even in these times, God, as he always does, shows up and delivers His children. He is the same yesterday, today, and forever. He can still deliver.

But, because we choose to leave Him out of the equation, we instead turn to worldly solutions like welfare as our only source.

Becoming a hand out rather than a hand up, welfare then invades our lives and becomes a generational curse. Nothing that the "system" gives you is going to produce long term wealth and stability for you or your family; Mother, grandmother, great-grandmother, all in the same household, no one having anything to show for their life. Where is the legacy for the children?

If you don't believe it, pick up any newspaper. The results are evident. Our children are crying out for our help. They are seeking love and family wherever they can find it; gangs, drugs, sex. We can no longer afford to blame all of the problems in our community on the "man". At some point, the problem becomes ours. If you're not willing to work at transforming the environment to meet your needs, then you shouldn't show up in a courtroom crying when your son or daughter is hauled off to jail for life. Where were you when the grades were slipping? Where were you when detention started? Where were you when the suspension was issued?

The system is a vicious cycle that has you caught in a never ending spiral. If you always do what you've always done, then you'll always get what you've always got. You will never arrive.

The widow of Zerephath was no stranger to lack. In fact, not only had she lost her husband, she lost one of her beloved sons. She had nothing left. Poverty and famine was all she had to look forward to. She had no entitlement programs, no social services worker, and no homeless shelter. She often starved herself to feed her remaining son. She found herself scraping the bottom of the barrel for flour so that she could make a morsel of bread for her and her son to eat. She began to prepare for their last supper.

As the widow prepared the meal, she heard a stranger call after her to bring him some water. The widow complied. Then, the stranger asked for some bread. The woman looked at him and told him that she had none. The stranger then said to her that she should prepare a cake and bring it to him. Once this was done, he said the woman should make something for herself and her son because God would not allow the flour to be used up or the oil to be run out until the He gave rain upon the land again.

The widow obeyed. Just as Elijah promised, the supply of oil and flour lasted until the rains came and revived the land. This deliverance is available, even today, if you are willing to listen and obey the will of God for your life.

Holding on to this belief kept me through the tough times.

The Ministry of Motherhood

It was Christmas Break. During my vacation my oldest son came down with the chicken pox. As was expected, my youngest son came down with the disease in exactly seven days. I took him to the clinic where I worked and had him seen by one of the pediatricians. She diagnosed him and gave me an excuse from work. I took the excuse and my son, full of bumps, to the office manager's office. She took the excuse and then I left.

I returned to work a week later, only to be relieved of my duties on Friday. The reason, I had abandoned my position. Even though the office manager had my work release, she refused to grant me my vacation days.

What a blow. I had worked for this company for five years. How would I support my family now? Where do I go? How do I find a job? *What do I do? I was troubled on every side, yet not disturbed; perplexed, but not in despair; persecuted, but not forsaken; and cast down, but not destroyed. (2 Corinthians 4:8-9)* Subjected to sin and suffering, I was never out of hope. God had not abandoned me. Christ demonstrated his power in and through me.

I was unable to get assistance, my husband would not pay child support, and my parents were doing all they could. But, God has a way of turning evil into good for those who love him.

Never having taught a day in my life, I pursued a position as an instructor. Much to my surprise, the school hired me on my first interview. The bottom line, when one door closes, another one will open. You simply need to take the steps necessary to move forward in your destiny.

God sees the needs of those who cannot help themselves. Intervening in very subtle ways, an unexpected check or a job that you really weren't trained for, God lets us know He understands we don't sometimes have the resources to get going. Triumphs for God explains what life is all about. Facing detours allows God to act as the Department of Transportation in our lives by repairing the crooked places and moving the road blocks away. All we have to do is sit in the passenger seat and let Him drive.

Whenever we become anxious about our circumstances, it is a misguided attempt to control the future. Mother's should rely on him daily for physical, emotional, and spiritual needs. Never believe that God does not care for you.

God is our best example of a good parent.
Give ear, O my people, to my law: incline your ears to the words of my mouth. I will open my mouth in a parable: I will utter dark sayings of old: Which we have heard and known, and our fathers have told us. We will not hide them from their children, shewing to the generation to come the praises of the LORD, and his strength, and his wonderful works that he hath done. For he established a testimony in Jacob, and appointed a law in Israel, which he commanded our fathers, that they should make them known to their children: That the generation to come

The Ministry of Motherhood

might know them, even the children which should be born; who should arise and declare them to their children: That they might set their hope in God, and not forget the works of God, but keep his commandments: And might not be as their fathers, a stubborn and rebellious generation; a generation that set not their heart aright, and whose spirit was not steadfast with God. (Psalms 78: 1-8)

These scriptures remind us that God praises, advises, nurtures, encourages, teaches, and trains us. Teaching our children to live a Christian life is the job of every mother. Communicating our expectations to our children with destructive criticism, lack of quality time, and dysfunctional marriages destroys the relationships between mothers and children. Emphasizing the right things in the right ways is our responsibility. Wholesome instruction and proper admonishment builds a strong foundation for future development. Material possessions only cloud the issue. Quality time is the best expression of your love because it assures your children they are important in your life. Reliable, trustworthy, patient, and compassionate attributes mirror the grace and mercy of God for His children, and therefore should be the foundation on which we build our parenting. Mothers should love sacrificially, like the mother in 1 Kings 3:26. Or Jochebed, Moses' mother who hid him for three months, and then had him released into the sea to be found and raised by the Egyptians so that he would not be killed.

"Sticks and Stones may break my bones but words will never hurt me," doesn't apply to parenting. Deflating your child's self worth with words will have a lasting effect on their lives. Telling your children they'll never amount to anything will only become a self-fulfilling prophecy. You have the power of life and death in your own tongue; speak peace, love, joy, and happiness into their lives. If you always say that your children are bad, then what do you expect them to be? Remind your children about what God says about them. Help them to see themselves through God's eyes. Placing your children's needs first will demonstrate to them their importance in your life, which will minimize their need to feel important to anyone else. Praying mothers who have a right relationship with God and lay hold on Him, can trust His promise that if you raise your child in the way they should go, when they are old they will not depart from it.. You are not perfect and expecting you to be perfect is not God's intention. In fact, the bible tells us that we have all sinned and come short of the glory of God. But, God can make up for the shortfall if we seek Him and His wisdom first.

A PRAYER FOR DELIVERANCE

Lord, Your name is Wonderful, Counselor, Mighty God, Everlasting Father, and the Prince of Peace.

Lord, I confess that everyone that reads this book and who is held captive by the bondage of laziness, slothfulness, low self esteem, and welfare abuse will be set free through Jesus Christ. Lord, remind them that we wrestle not against flesh and blood, but against powers and principalities in high places. I declare that they will put on the whole armor of God and fight the good fight against the strongholds in their lives. I declare that they will be strong in You so that they can be delivered from the enemy. I command addictions, ungodly habits, and strongholds to be broken, In Jesus' name. Lord, heal every emotional and psychological wound and restore their self confidence and self worth. Give them the desires of their heart as they delight in You. Create in them a clean heart and renew a steadfast spirit within them. Bring them to a place of understanding where they can recognize the work of evil and cry to You for help. Remind them that You have begun a good work in them and You will complete it.

Forgive them for all acts of sinfulness. Forgive them for relying on themselves instead of on You. Lord, remind them to forgive those that have harmed them.

Lead them not into temptation, but deliver them from the evil one.

O Lord, our Lord, how excellent is Your name in all the earth. Your mercy endures forever. Yours is the kingdom and the power and the glory forever and ever, amen.

CHAPTER FOUR

"PK's (Preachers Kids)"

1 Timothy 3:4-5 He must manage his own household well, with all dignity keeping his children submissive, 5 for if someone does not know how to manage his own household, how will he care for God's church?

Answering the call of God is a personal decision on the part of every minister, pastor, teacher, or evangelist. Rarely do any of these clergy consult their children about their calling. So, why is it that society propels children from ministerial families into some never never land of perfection? If I heard it once, I heard it a million times: "Preachers kids are the worst." How on earth did people arrive at that conclusion?

Being a PK (Preacher's kid for those not familiar with the vernacular) is tough. All eyes are on you. The expectations and demands, whether real or perceived, are almost unbearable at times. It's not that our behavior is any worse than other children. The problem is people pull out the microscope when it comes to PK's.

Spending the first fifteen years of my life trying to live up to those expectations at all costs made me a great student; a regular on the honor roll. If I received less than a perfect score on anything, I took it upon myself to work extra hard the next time. On any given day, you could find me immersed in a book. Finishing first in class always dismayed my teachers because when I was done, I wanted to talk to the other kids and tell them what they were doing wrong. Furthering my travels into "geekdom", my mother subsequently told the teachers to send me to the library when I was done.

Entrepreneurship was a gift I embraced early on as I hand made pom-poms for the girls' sneakers and sold them for one dollar each.

Church participation was a given; the choir, the Baptist Training Union, and every Easter and Christmas play or pageant known to mankind. I was on my way to proving the cynics wrong. I would not be the worst kid simply because my father was a pastor. How could anyone possibly believe that I could be a bad kid?

The Ministry of Motherhood

Until...

It was 1982, and the school year began like any other. I was involved in all my regular activities; booster club, student council, school choir, church choir; and any other activities that would look good in a college portfolio. I even ran track, not because I really liked it, but because it would look good.

Then came this smooth talkin', good lookin', chocolate-covered ladies man. All the girls wanted him. I had actually seen many girls fight for his affections, all the time wondering what the fuss was all about. He wanted me. Maybe because he felt like I was untouchable, or maybe because he felt like I would be a good conquest, I really don't know which, but the fact remains that he turned on the charm and pursued me relentlessly. Ultimately, he was playing a game. A game he had no intentions of losing. I was the prize.

Flattered by the attention, I really didn't have time for a relationship. Meeting the high expectations that had been placed on me was the only thing on my mind.

Rejection for someone who loved themselves more than they could ever love anyone else was not an option easily explored. Yet, my initial lack of returned affections only made him more determined. He wanted control of the situation and he would do anything to get it.

It should be noted here that until this point, for the most part, I had always been obedient to my parents. Their word was LAW. I had always tried to do what they told me. No questions asked. Of course, I was determined to stay the course.

This young man's initial advances toward me went unanswered for a long time. I had been resilient in my efforts to resist him; until the fateful day when my mother relented and decided to let him take me out.

Giving in to my new beau's request for a date was difficult for my mother. Friendship with his parents and church membership were his only saving graces. Naturally, she believed that it would be okay for us to spend time together.

Doing all the right things, asking for permission to take me out, and, in the beginning, he worked extra hard at getting me home on time all painted a beautiful picture. Any parent would be proud to have their daughter go out with such a wonderful young man. Hiding beneath the surface, however, was a darker picture that wouldn't be displayed until it had been sold to the buyer; me. The darkness of his soul crept out little by little; insidious, vague, and dangerous.

Being naïve in the department of male-female relationships, I was immediately smitten by his suave attitude and charming demeanor. Knowing exactly what to say, he spoke often of church and God. In fact, he even professed at some point in our relationship that he had been called into the ministry. He paid attention to all the things that I liked to do and he showered me with what I perceived to be love. Like a moth to a flame, I was drawn into his deceit.

The Ministry of Motherhood

Determined, however, not to be swayed, I held onto my convictions for a long time.

This was true love as I had imagined it. I couldn't speak his name without getting goose bumps and butterflies. My heart would skip a beat whenever he entered the room. Being challenged finally to prove that I love him, I had come to a crossroad.

Matthew 7:13 Enter through the narrow gate. For wide is the gate and broad is the road that leads to destruction, and many enter through it. I was no exception. I entered the wide gate.

CHAPTER FIVE

"Innocence Lost"

Proverbs 2: 10-12 When wisdom enters your heart, and knowledge is pleasant to your soul, discretion will preserve you, understanding will keep you, to deliver you from the way of evil, from the man who speaks perverse things.

It was nearing my sixteenth birthday, I had gone on a trip with my father and his family. We were participants in the Baptist Sunday School Convention. The entire time I was there, I can remember writing letters and postcards to send home to my boyfriend.

My step-sister was there and so was a family friend. We spent each evening well into the wee hours of the morning talking about boys and sex. Our family friend seemed to have all the answers.

Two weeks after our return, my sixteenth birthday finally arrived. There had been talk of a sweet sixteen party, but it didn't happen, so my boyfriend asked to take me out for a special evening. My mother agreed and we were off.

The evening was warm and balmy, much like every other evening in Texas' summers. At least a soft, southerly breeze was blowing. This made it feel cooler than it really was. The stars were plentiful. The moon hanging like a smile in the night sky made this the kind of night that astrologers loved because it appeared that each star could be identified by name.

We went to dinner at a nice restaurant and saw a movie. Then, he showered me with kind words and expressions of love. What more could a girl ask for?

"Baby, I love you," he said and I melted. "You mean the world to me. You know I'm gonna marry you so, if we get together tonight, it'll be okay."

Understanding the innuendo, I began to imagine what a night of love making would be like. Abruptly, this thought left my mind as I could see my mothers face before my eyes looking at me with disappointment. Still, I moved forward without hesitation.

Before I knew it, I was at the LaQuinta Inn. "What are we doing here," I naively questioned, knowing intuitively what my boyfriend expected.

The Ministry of Motherhood

"I have something special planned," he seductively replied.

Romanticizing in my adolescent mind about his thoughtfulness at taking me to a hotel, I was floating effortlessly on cloud nine. Crispy, white linen that crackled when you laid on them, a television nestled in a cherry wood armoire, two low back arm chairs covered in burgundy leather fabric with a hint of cherry wood peaking out beneath, made this hotel room similar to any other. The special feeling that I had came from being there with him.

After sitting there for a while, he started to nibble on my neck. The nibbling quickly became kissing and the kissing turned into touching, and before long, feelings began to invade my body that I had never experienced before. I never thought in my wildest dreams I could feel so good. This was more than I could ever have imagined.

I was tingling all over. My body got hot and wet all at the same time. I was consumed with lust and it felt so good. We were doing things that no good Christian girl should ever imagine doing. My mind kept saying no, but my body was certainly telling me yes.

When things were about as hot as they could get, I remember my boyfriend saying breathlessly, "You know you're gonna get pregnant."

With what little strength I had left, I declared with much conviction, "I don't care."

Where did that come from? Was I out of my mind? Had some alien invader taken over my body and began speaking for me? Where did Cheryl go and who was that fool who didn't care about getting pregnant?

That had to have been the case because I could feel what seemed to be my eyes rolling back in my head as my body began to convulse as if I were having an epileptic seizure.

A sense of excitement grew inside me like nothing I had ever known. My heart pounded, my body twitched, my toes curled; pure ecstasy. The harder he pushed, the harder I pushed back, and then it was over.

I had given myself to him completely and nothing would separate us, or so I thought. We were joined by a special bond that could not be broken. This man had ravished my body and claimed my heart all at one time.

I remember he was extremely happy as he made the most unfounded statement. "You know you're pregnant," he said without missing a beat.

In my foolish frame of mind, I giggled and said, "That's okay."

In reality, I really didn't believe that it could happen to me. I believed that this brief walk on the wild side wouldn't hurt.

What they say about your first love is true. Once we made love, I had created a soul tie that would prove to be difficult to break. What I felt for him increased a hundred fold that evening.

OPEN DOOR POLICY

I Kings 3:9 So give your servant a discerning heart to govern your people and to distinguish between right and wrong. For who is able to govern this great people of yours?

Having an open door policy can lead to dark corners where Satan is most assuredly lurking. Mistakenly, as Christians we believe every door of opportunity is opened by God. Continually reminding ourselves the enemy has become adept at making things that are not good for us look good to us, will keep us from walking through doors that lead to temptation. When we are not fully in connection with God, we can be fooled by wolves in sheep's clothing. Always seeking to devour us the author of all lies and deception, predicates his plans on making us lose sight of

God's purpose for our lives. Finding our life's partner is one area where the devil makes his presence known. Understanding our need for companionship, our need for love, and our need to be needed, Satan weaves a web of lies so intricate that we are unable to easily free ourselves from its grip. Remembering to ask God for His guidance when we are seeking a mate, will help us to secure long lasting, meaningful marriages. A mate truly sent by God will want to do those things that are pleasing to Him as much as we do. Youthful ignorance caused me to be fooled by this trick of the enemy. My wolf in sheep's clothing declared his unequivocal love for God and his call into the ministry as he huffed and puffed and blew my house down, until I was left unsheltered from the storm that lay ahead.

As women, we need to be mindful of the fact that our bodies are a temple of God. Refusing to give our bodies away freely will eliminate the creation of soul ties that can be difficult, if not impossible, to break.

Asking God for discernment as we make decisions in our lives keeps us from wasting valuable time as we move toward our purpose in life. Moving on matters of importance should always be done according to God's will for our lives.

Whenever in doubt, ask yourself, "Is what I am about to do scriptural? Would God be pleased?"

The Ministry of Motherhood

If the answer is no, then you should reconsider your decision. Following this model will always lead to a better outcome.

A PRAYER FOR DISCERNMENT

You alone are holy. There is none like You. It is You that we have our trust. We exalt You, we adore You, and we lift You up so that all men might be drawn unto You.

Fill us with the fear of the Lord. Give us wisdom for every decision that we make. Help us to seek Your truth. Lord, give us the spirit of discernment to make decisions based on Your revelation. Help us to make godly choices and keep us from doing anything foolish. Help us to listen to godly council and not be un-teachable. Help us to lean not to our own understanding, but in all our ways acknowledge You. Help us to hear the call that you have on our lives. Help us to realize who we are and whose we are. Remind us of our higher purpose. Don't let us get sidetracked with things that are unessential to Your purpose. Help us to rise above our circumstances so that we can see Your purpose for our lives. Help us to wait on Your perfect timing. We will seek You for direction and hear when You speak to our souls.

Lord, forgive us not seeking You first as we make decisions for our lives. Forgive for not listening when we hear You speak to hearts, and for turning a deaf ear on Your Word. Help us to forgive those who have trespassed against us.

Lead us not into temptation, but deliver us from the evil one.

You are the one true living God, the Lord eternal, the holy one. You alone are worthy to be praised. In Jesus' name we pray, Amen.

CHAPTER SIX

"The Abyss"

1 John 4:16 We have known and believed the love that God has for us. God is love, and He who abides in love abides in God, and God in him.

When I found out I was pregnant, I wasn't sure about anything anymore. I was sixteen and certainly too young to have a baby by society's standards. What's worse, I was a PK. Oh my God! I guess everyone was right. Preacher's kids are the worse. We always mess up with no way out the devastation that I felt was unexplainable. I felt like I was in a bottomless pit looking up. To this day, I don't think anyone really knows how low I felt; the guilt, the shame, the agony. I wasn't upset about carrying a child. In fact, I loved my baby very much. But, concern about what other people would think was what consumed my thoughts. All of my efforts had been in vain. I knew no one would remember the good student I had been, or the memory verses I cited by heart. They wouldn't remember all of the sweet melodies I sang each Sunday in church, or the fact that I was on the fast track for graduation a year early. All anyone would remember was that I was a preacher's daughter, I was pregnant, and I was unmarried.

On the phone and completely out of breath from crying, I told my boyfriend he was about to be a father.

He actually took it quite well. I thought he would blow up or start cussing. Instead, he began to make plans to tell his parents. I guess he was right. He knew all along I would become pregnant that night.

He even mentioned marriage. Not sure at that point that marriage was an option, I was glad to know that at least at this point he was willing to "do the right thing."

Telling my Father was a different story. I don't know why, but this made me very afraid. I guess little girls have a special affinity for their fathers.

Once my father arrived, the tears began to flow down my cheeks on their all too familiar path. I became so emotional I couldn't tell him the news on my own. Time stood still as my

The Ministry of Motherhood

mother began the conversation. My heart plummeted into the pit of my stomach like a fallen rock from the top of the highest cliff. Traveling a million miles away, my mind could only register the movement of my mother's lips. I didn't hear or comprehend a word she was saying.

My anxiety about telling him proved to be unwarranted. He took the news a lot better than I thought he would. Praise God! I was sure he would erupt like a volcano and consume everyone around him in the molten lava. Instead, he and my mother vowed to help me get through this no matter what: A true, "Thank you, Jesus" moment.

Continuing my studies at school until it was time for me to deliver my son was difficult. My mother was adamant I not be shipped off to some special school for pregnant girls. I was in a program geared toward the medical professions and she didn't want me to lose any ground.

My mother spoke to any school official that would listen; the teachers, the counselor, the principal, the superintendent, anyone. Having a pregnant girl in class was different. They tried to come up with reasons why I should leave the school.

"She is a bad example for the other girls," they said. "She is a liability risk. She will not be able to keep up in her condition."

One teacher and a school counselor were in my corner. They advocated on my behalf every chance they got.

In the final analysis, their arguments proved to be groundless. Finally, the decision was made. If special needs children could be matriculated into a regular classroom, then so could I. After all, pregnancy is a natural part of life. I had just gotten to it a bit earlier than most. Relenting, the school allowed me to stay and finish my studies until graduation.

CHAPTER SEVEN

"Mama's Sermon"

Genesis 3:16 Then he said to the woman, I will sharpen the pain of your pregnancy, and in pain you will give birth.

I went to the doctor several times with what I thought were labor pains. The last time I visited, the nurse said in a quiet, calming voice, "When the real ones hit, you'll know it." Boy, was she right! I think someone once said that the pains are like taking your bottom lip and pulling it over your head. I agree. Gimme drugs!

When the first pain hit, a flood of emotions came all at once; insecurity, fear, frustration. It was all so overwhelming. We made it to the hospital in record time. The nurse checked me in and wheeled me to the delivery area. When I heard the blood curdling screams from the other room, I almost wet my pants. I wanted to turn back, but it was too late. Making matters worse, the nurse came toward me with a needle that looked like it was as long as an unsharpened pencil.

"Where are you goin' with that," I asked.

"This is your epidural. It will stop the pain," she said.

Maybe I should revisit this gimme drugs thing, I thought.

Remembering I read somewhere epidurals could cause you to be paralyzed, paranoia began to set in. I tried to be a big girl, but deep down inside I was petrified. Delivering a baby was truly a woman's job.

As always, my mother was right there with me every step of the way. Curled up in the corner of the room, I could see her face from the corner of my eye. It was wrinkled up like a prune as she stood grunting with each grueling push that I made.

We made eye contact, but we never said a word. We didn't have to. Her face said it all. Her calling to the ministry of motherhood had come full circle. Her baby was now having a baby. Her display of love on this day was like a sermon: Its title; "Unconditional love." It's message, love endures all things, would stay with me all the days of my life.

The most important person in my life, my mother, remarried when I was seven years old,

The Ministry of Motherhood

but she always took full responsibility for my sister and me. The thing I love most about her is her faith in God. I loved sitting beside her when I was a little girl and listening to her tell stories about her childhood and the Bible. I know most of them by heart. When she tells a story, she always has a captive audience. It's at these moments her strength and faith are at their best. Exposing her life struggles and disappointments, I learned why she believed God no matter what. Her faith is the foundation I stood on when I became a mother. It is the foundation I stand on now. Clinging to it when life gets hard, my Mama's faith is the weapon that I have learned to use.

Experiencing childbirth made me grow up a lot. After my son was born, it was my mother who brought him to me. Taking one look at him, just as I did his brother years later, made me consider what type of life they would lead. I thought about whom they were and who they would become. I dreamed for them. I hoped for them. I prayed for them. I held them in my arms and I visualized the life they would live and the lives they would touch. Would they become doctors, lawyers, teachers? Or would they be dropouts living on welfare. When I looked at them, I counted more than fingers and toes, I counted the people they would become some day.

I realized everything concerning them depended on the sermon my life would preach. Each scripture would be written by the words I spoke, the experiences I encountered, and the circumstances I overcame. As each chapter unfolded, I was determined it would have a happy ending. Their births were the Genesis and if Revelation was to end triumphantly, I needed to be their savior here on Earth.

It's amazing how you don't really remember the pain once the baby gets here. It's such a miraculous event that you instantly forget all the agony.

With a marriage proposal still on the table and intent on doing the right thing, I hurriedly said yes.

We were relentless in pursuing my mother for her consent of this union because I was still a minor and I ignored her continuous pleas with me about marrying at such an early age. Pitfalls that most surely lay ahead were displayed in Technicolor as her words painted a bleak picture of my future. Self centered like any other teenager, I was convinced I needed to act more grown up than I was. I pretended the prospects of no steady income and no roof of my own didn't bother me. Playing a mental ping pong game trying to rationalize my situation with what I knew was right, only managed to confuse me even more. I had all the answers. She didn't know what she was talking about. She couldn't, or could she? Besides, my boyfriend and I loved each other and that's all we needed, right?

Reluctantly, my mother consented to the marriage and we immediately we began making arrangements. The ceremony would need to happen quickly because my fiancée had enlisted in the army. Clinging to the idea the army

The Ministry of Motherhood

would be our ticket to financial freedom, he would be shipped off to boot camp soon.

My father agreed to conduct the ceremony and we had the wedding at my mother's house. The whole idea was charming and romantic, but if I had been a believer in signs, Hurricane Alicia would have been a good one.

You see, Hurricane Alicia had just blown through our city and the aftermath was still very much evident. Some would've believed this was a sign not to get married. In my romantic stupor, I believed it was a sign we could whether any storm.

The wedding was simple. No guest list boasting two hundred plus guests, no grand church with stained glass windows and cushioned pews, no catered reception at the Hyatt Regency Hotel, and no long flowing dress with a train as long as the aisle. Just a matron of honor, a best man, and some close friends and family, including our son.

I wore a simple, off white suit and carried a dozen red roses down the hallway of my mother's modest three bedroom home . My fiancée wore a black suit with a crisp white shirt and a smile to match the occasion.

The reception was held right there at the house. No fancy food, no cake, just a few hors'd'oerves and some punch.

After the wedding, my new husband and I consummated our marriage in a beautiful hotel, the only honeymoon that we could afford. Like Cinderella, I was in a fairytale; champagne, beautiful music, beautiful surroundings.

The evening went exactly as planned. The intimacy we experienced was every bit as wonderful as what we had experienced before. Besides, we were legal now. That made it all the more sweet.

The very next morning, my new husband was whisked away in an army issued vehicle to begin his experience in boot camp.

Ending in a few short months, boot camp was finally over and my husband sent for me.

Our initial encounter would make the soap operas blush. We ran into one another's arms as if it had been years since we were together. My ex had a flair for the dramatic, so each moment was intense and electrifying. The living quarters we were in were small, but it didn't matter because for most of the weekend we were attached like Siamese twins.

Leaving for home was somewhat of a let down because I was once again separating from the love of my life. Soon, however, my spirits would be uplifted by the news that we were expecting our second bundle of joy.

Convincing me to leave school and move with him to Fort Campbell, Kentucky allowed my husband to secure an extra stipend when my son and I arrived. We lived off base and everything sounded wonderful, but, as with anything else, it was too good to be true.

Anxiety overtook me like a rushing wind as I recognized I would be living away from home for the first time. Yet, without hesitation, I packed my bags and moved to be with my husband. No driver's license, a husband, a son, and a "bun in

The Ministry of Motherhood

the oven," I was a little girl pretending to be a grown woman.

HAPPILY EVER AFTER

Proverbs 30:21-23 "Under three things the earth trembles, under four it cannot bear up; an unloved woman who is married.

Marriage is not a step to be taken lightly. As little girls, we spend much of our time daydreaming about our wedding day, but we rarely think about what it takes to maintain a marriage; the ups, the downs, the good, the bad. We spend more time preparing for the wedding than we do preparing for the marriage. Getting married is easy, building a marriage is difficult.

When each person in the relationship goes to their respective home at the end of the day, courtship is a breeze. Learning to live with someone else's faults, on the other hand, can be very difficult, if not impossible, to do. Basing a marriage on superficial ideals is detrimental.

Maintaining "happily ever after" is difficult because each person in the marriage brings a wealth of experience from their family of origin. Beliefs about child rearing, financial management, and employment expectations are all formed as we grow into adulthood. Combining these ideas into a workable relationship can be hard. Communicating about these differences before marriage can save you from heartache in the end. Compromise will be essential to making the relationship work.

Examining what we want in a mate will help us to learn more about ourselves. Materialism should never be a key factor for marriage. Listing external characteristics as opposed to internal ones could expose us as superficial, shallow beings. Emotional connection, companionship, and love should be the driving forces that lead us to a mate with whom we can spend the rest of our lives.

Women, we should look at ourselves as well. Are we deserving of a mate sent by God? Are we striving to be Proverbs 31 women? Can we be the wife Ephesians calls for? Remember submission? Is that word in your vocabulary? If not, then you need to go back to the drawing board for yourself as well. Finding the right partner is not as important as being the right person. Don't be pressured into marriage. Be willing to wait.

The Ministry of Motherhood

We should ask ourselves if the mate we are looking for is scriptural. Would God approve of this kind of man? Ephesians and Proverbs give us guidelines as to what this man should look like. If your man does not exhibit some of these traits, then he is not of God and you need to go back to the drawing board. Simply being a Christian doesn't make a man an appropriate partner either.

Believing someone else can complete you is a mistake. Only God can complete you. Each individual must enter the marriage as a whole person. If not, the person seeking to be completed will be reduced to a second class citizen.

As a minister of motherhood, it is important to understand a dysfunctional marriage can result in dysfunctional children. Children need to be given credit for their uncanny ability to sense when things are not quite right. Staying in a loveless marriage, an abusive marriage, or an otherwise dysfunctional marriage will only make matters worse for the children. They will grow up believing dysfunction is the norm.. They will internalize attributes that will filter into their own marriages; anger, distrust, poor judgment. Don't sentence your children to a life of dysfunction. The benefits may not outweigh the outcome.

CHAPTER EIGHT

"The Cycle Begins"

Psalm 91:1-2 He who dwells in the secret place of the Most High shall abide under the shadow of the Almighty. I will say of the Lord, "He is my refuge and my fortress; my God, in Him I will trust.

Having a refuge and a fortress is exactly what I needed when I got to Fort Campbell Kentucky. Isolated and alone, far from my family and my friends, I had only God to turn to.

Initial impressions of Kentucky and the military life were not very remarkable. Cold, isolated, and desolate, the grass looked like hay and everywhere I turned there was nothing but

land. We had completely left civilization and the only sign of life were the people on the base.
Having nothing on a foreign country, army bases are a whole new world.

The very first meeting we attended on the base discussed the stresses of an army family. Drugs were in demand and much to my surprise, one of the first lessons we learned as a new military family dealt with how to deal with the rampant drug activity on the base. This country's government, the armed forces, and the people in them were above reproach: Right? Alcoholism, drug abuse, and domestic violence go hand in hand with being a part of the military. A very lonely place set apart from the world, our town home and the base itself could've been in Alaska. We didn't have transportation, so getting around was very difficult. Taxi service in an old beat up station wagon was our only mode of transportation. Spending most of my days taking care of my son and reading allowed me to get my first glimpse of what single parenting was all about. The isolation was an early sign of domestic violence.

I had always heard the army was no place for a black man. I must concur. I will always believe in my heart the army changes people. My husband was no exception. Somehow, he disappeared into the rank and file. The stories of "be all you can be" only applied to certain people. The army may be the place where boys go to become men, but what kind of men do they become?

The Ministry of Motherhood

One evening, my husband invited some of his army buddies to our home. We sat and chatted about various and sundry things. The time went by almost in obscurity. Surprisingly, when our guests left, my husband began ranting and raving about how I was trying to entice the men he had invited. Confused and amazed, I started thinking about how just a few months earlier I was flattered he wanted me all to himself.

The entire night he kept screaming about how my leg shook back and forth in a tantalizing motion. He believed this was some sort of invitation for sex. I was very pregnant. I didn't even want him. How could he believe I wanted someone else?

Escalating into physical confrontation, first a push, then a shove, and before long a slap, to the face that left me stunned and in shock, the sting from the open handed lick he had inflicted felt like a million ants biting me at one time. I didn't know whether to run or cry. I did both.

Running up the stairs, my husband giving chase the entire way, I was afraid of what he might do if he caught me. I was even more afraid for my unborn child.

I locked myself in my oldest son's room. I sat on the bed holding him as I listened to his father frantically trying to open the door.

Physical abuse was not something I was accustomed to. Even as a child, I rarely experienced any form of physical punishment.

Entering the room charging like a tiger released from a cage, my husband grabbed me and pushed me to the floor. That night, he injured my soul more than he injured my body. Knowing that my father never beat me, I resolved neither would my husband. Fighting back with everything I had in me, pregnancy was the last thing on my mind. This was the first physical attack I remember, but it was definitely not the last.

The next day I awoke to, "I'm sorry. You know I love you, right? You know I didn't mean to hurt you. You're my Babe."

Becoming the endearing, charming, loving man that I had married, complete with flowers and dinner, he was very apologetic about the whole ordeal. So, the cycle began.

My husband found my pain an outlet for his misery. Verbal confrontations were frequent, but physical ones were the worse. Despite the continuous cycle, I naively chose to ignore my husband was quickly slipping away.

Awakened from my denial when my husband asked me to pawn the wedding rings my father bought, (that's right, even the rings that betrothed me to him were paid for by my father) I questioned my decision to get married.

I don't remember the excuse that he gave for needing the money. Volatility increased as time went by, so did his time away from home. Actually, this was a good thing because it meant he wouldn't have time to find something to become angry about.

Dysfunctional though it was, there were still times when his presence would have made all the difference in the world.

The Ministry of Motherhood

It was around midnight. My oldest son was running a fever of 104. His father was no where to be found. Transportation was difficult to come by and the base was at least five miles away.

I was very pregnant by this time. Getting around was not an easy task. I called a taxi and waited for its arrival. With my son in my arms, I proceeded to the base hospital where we were met by the nurse on call. The doctor was very kind and provided my son with the best of care.
"Are you in the military?" the doctor asked.
"No," I responded.
"Where's your husband?"
"I really don't know."

Suddenly, I felt very apprehensive about the whole line of questioning and the doctor must've sensed this because he stopped asking questions and proceeded to give me a prescription for my son.
During the early morning hours, my husband finally returned home.
"Where were you?" I asked with contempt in my voice.
"None of your damn business," he replied.
"Our son is upstairs sick and all you have to say is none of your damn business?" I shouted.

I really don't know what had gotten in to me that night. What I do know is my children have always been a source of courage for me. I guess that's what they mean when they say children are given to you not only for what you can do for them, but for what they can do for you. I really didn't care about the outcome of the argument, I simply wanted it to be known that my children were the most important thing in my life and no one and nothing would ever change that.

My husband must've seen something that night also, because to my surprise, he didn't pursue the fight. Instead, he was very sorry for what he had done. He promised it would never happen again.

It was the same old song, different tune. I let it go and didn't add fuel to the fire.

I knew my days would be numbered at Fort Campbell. The isolation and the rollercoaster of emotions were way too much for me to handle. There are some that would argue I should've stayed in the marriage for the benefits, but I can't imagine any benefits worth my dignity, my self worth, and my very soul.

Growing up in abusive and otherwise dysfunctional homes leads far too many children to become abusers or to be abused themselves. Many express their inability to control the situation through anger, lack of discipline and self control, or self destructive, demoralizing behaviors like substance abuse, sexual deviance, and violence. Still others become critical, judgmental, overbearing, and overachievers with an inability to truly express or experience love. Affection is lost on them and their ability to express affection is severely impacted. Hiding behind a façade of having it all together, the truth is on the inside they always remain the child that was forced to live in a situation they could not control.

The Ministry of Motherhood

    Refusing to allow my children to grow up this way, I knew when the opportunity presented itself I would leave my husband.

I felt guilty about the decision I made to leave him. Always fixing what he had done to me, he knew how to relieve the pain and in my mind, I wanted to help him overcome his demons. I believed I could fix him. Uncertainty and confusion vexed my soul.

DOMESTIC VIOLENCE

Anguish and solitude are two words that very fittingly describe the feelings left behind by domestic violence. Feeling separated from people, life, and even God, the abuse suffered can cause you to toss yourself into the cesspool of desperation. You begin to long for better times, yet, you're left with the understanding that life will never be the same. The very act threatens your soul. The disappointment and disillusionment experienced because of the betrayal of the perpetrator poisons your thinking and your feelings. It threatens your ability to live life abundantly.

Going against the second greatest commandment, "Love thy neighbor as thyself," violence is rendered in compatible with love.

The fruits of the spirit are love, kindness, and gentleness. Therefore, the Holy Spirit is grieved when domestic violence occurs. Ephesians further admonishes husbands to love their wives unconditionally, and sacrificially.

Making the ultimate sacrifice for you, God has demonstrated the value He places on your life. God wants you to be loved.

No one has authority to make you feel less than a person. If you are in a relationship where you are abused physically, psychologically, emotionally, or financially, you should ask God for guidance. His will for us is that we should be in good health and prosper, even as our souls prosper. You need to bring your life into alignment with God's perfect will.

Holding all these ideals together is faith. Through faith, the pain of domestic violence comes as a unique opportunity to glorify God because we can rest assured in the end that all things work together for good to them that love God.

A PRAYER FOR VICTIMS OF ABUSE

Lord God, You are great and greatly to be praised. Who can be compared with You in the heavens above or in the earth beneath? Great and glorious is Your name, O God most high.

Father, I ask you to replace sadness with joy, defeat with victory, and fear with love, power, and a sound mind. Help those who feel victimized or sad not to focus on their circumstances, but rather to focus on Your blessings in their lives. Remind them that Your thoughts for them are thoughts of good and not of evil, to give them a future and a hope. Lord God, help them to not be conformed to this world, but transformed by the renewing of their minds. I declare that they will not entertain confusion in their minds, but will live with clarity.

Lord, Your son, Jesus, turned water into wine, made a blind man see, and a lame man walk. He healed all manners of disease and even raised the dead. You are the same yesterday, today, and forever. With You all things are possible. I decree and declare that You will bring about a healing of the mind for those who are in need of deliverance. I declare that these persons will be set free. Their strongholds will be torn down and their breakthrough is on the way. Whatever things are true, noble, just, pure, lovely, of good report, having virtue, or anything praiseworthy let them think on these things.

Father, forgive them for doubting Your Word and your works. Lord, restore in them the joy of Your salvation. Lord, help them to forgive those that have placed their minds, bodies and spirits in turmoil.

To You alone, God, goes all the glory and the honor. You, O God, are Jehovah Niesi, the God of our victory. All that is in heaven and earth is Yours. In Jesus' name, Amen.

CHAPTER TEN

"Doing the Right Thing"

Psalms 1:1 Blessed is the man that walketh not in the counsel of the ungodly, nor stands in the path of sinners, nor sits in the seat of the scornful.

The opportunity to leave came sooner rather than later. My husband's parents purchased a vehicle for us in Texas. We needed to go home so we could drive the car back to Kentucky. Without a second thought, I began packing everything that I could. We were going home and I planned to stay. The excitement was almost more than I could handle. The trip to Texas was a blur to me. All I wanted was to see was the sign that said welcome to The Lone Star State. I knew in my heart I would never set foot back into Fort Campbell, Kentucky. If I could just make it back to Mama, my best example of real motherhood, I would be okay.

When we finally made it to Houston, the trip seemed worthwhile. We visited my husband's parents first so we could pick up the car they purchased for us. Our last and final stop was with my parents. When my husband began packing to go back to the base, I told him that I would not be returning. Searching for a reason to stay, I used my impending delivery.

Armed with the support of my family, he knew he had no choice but to return to the base alone.

Ambivalent feelings resurfaced as my husband departed for the base. I was a single woman who just happened to be married. Feeling alone in my marriage was natural. Parenting alone was even more natural. Having no real male influence for my children was troubling, but their father's influence would be detrimental. It's sad to say, but there are times when no male influence is better than a negative male influence. Plus, my father and step father were always nearby. Growing up believing that violence was a way of life was not what I wanted for my boys.

It's been said that the lack of male role models in a boy's life can lead to juvenile delinquency, poor school performance, and other socio-economic problems. But, what is one to do, when the male role model refuses to behave like

The Ministry of Motherhood

a man? A mother does what she has to do to protect her children. If that means depriving them of a father who is abusive, distant, and unconcerned, then leaving is what you do, right? I don't know the real answer. What I do know is my children's lives were more peaceful, more content, and well rounded, while the siblings with whom their father lived were plagued with constant police intervention and turmoil. I know I did the right thing.

A PRAYER FOR GODLY RELATIONSHIPS

Lord, We thank You for You are good and Your love endures forever. In You I trust, O my God. Lord, I thank You for fellowship and communion.

Father, I confess that those persons who read this book will have good, godly relationships where they can openly share their heart. I pray that these relationships will be with Titus 2 women, trustworthy women who will speak the truth into their lives and not just say what they want to hear. I declare that they will not walk in the counsel of the ungodly or stand in the path of sinners, nor sit in the seat of the scornful; but we delight in Your word. I confess that they will surround themselves with those who are positioned to help them glorify

You. Arm them with Your word. Help them to be doers and not just hearers of Your word.

Lord, I ask that You align their relationships with Your Word. Help them to be obedient as You order their steps. I declare that the Holy Spirit give them discernment to separate themselves from their gossip buddies, their smoking buddies, their promiscuous buddies, their club hopping buddies, and anyone who the devil may use to keep them from glorifying God.

Lord, forgive them for sin. Forgive them for unrighteous relationships that keep them from living the lives that You have planned for them. Forgive them for disobedience when You have told them to cut certain relationships off, yet, they have refused to do so. Remind us to forgive others.

Lead us not into temptation, but deliver us from the evil one.

For Yours is the kingdom, and the power, and the glory, forever. Amen.

CHAPTER ELEVEN

"Control"

Isaiah 1: 19-20 If you are willing and obedient, you shall eat the good of the land; but if you refuse and rebel, you shall be devoured by the sword; for the mouth of the Lord has spoken.

Devoured by the sword for refusing to follow instruction and rebelling against everything I had been taught made coming home difficult for me but, I was finally home. Love and support were invaluable, but I couldn't shake the feeling that maybe I hadn't given marriage all I had. After all, we had only been together in the same household for a short time. Maybe I hadn't been as supportive of my husband as I should've been. He was young, and it must've been difficult to support a family and deal with the stresses of being in the army.

No matter, I was at home now and I needed to begin making a life for myself and my children.

Getting a job alleviated some of my doubts. At least now I was a viable part of the equation.

When I married my husband, I thought not working would be a good thing because I could spend all of my time with my children. Unknowingly, I had fallen into one of the pitfalls of abuse. It was called control. The control belonged to my husband. If he didn't want to buy groceries, he didn't have to. If he didn't want to pay for school, he didn't have to. The fate of our entire family was in his hands.

With my new job, I was now on the road to a career and I was determined to make it work. The pay was not great, but I was in a field that I loved; medicine. Getting financial support from my husband would prove to be difficult.

Someone, I don't remember who, told me if I contacted the Red Cross and told them my situation, they would relay the information to my husband's commanding officer (CO) and he would see to it that I get what I needed to take care of myself and my children. Well, she was right. As a matter of fact, I learned that he was still receiving money for the "family" even though we were no longer in Kentucky. Speaking with the CO was a great move. The checks began to arrive shortly thereafter. It was around this same time that I began to receive

The Ministry of Motherhood

phone calls from my husband. Convincingly, he started to tell me how much he missed me. I wonder now if he missed me or the money.

He pleaded with me to return to the base, but I held my ground. There was no way I would return to that horrible place. The voices in my head returned. Had I betrayed him by leaving him when he needed me? Was he really sorry for what he had done? Had he learned his lesson while I was away? My defenses were down and despite my mother's best efforts, I was beginning to buy into his pleas. Love and forgiveness are God like qualities to have. Aren't they?

Heated arguments about my husband became the norm for my mother and me. Warning me continuously about my husband's empty promises didn't stop me from pleading his case with her. I found myself resenting my mother. I saw her efforts as deliberate sabotage of my attempts at being a woman. My husband's welfare and well-being had overtaken my thoughts. Didn't she know how much I loved this man? Wasn't she a Christian who believed in turning the other cheek?

How wrong was I? My mother was trying to spare me the pain and suffering that so many women experience at the hands of a boy pretending to be a man. Escaping what I perceived as my mother's negativity, the constant ridicule from my mother became increasingly more difficult.

Being discharged from the army was my husband's new plan for us to be together.

"Write a letter to the army commander. Tell him that my being in the army is placing a strain on our marriage," my husband said and continued. "This way, we can be together and I can take care of you and the boys."

"Are you sure this is the best idea?" I asked, feeling uncertain about his return home.

"You love me, don't you?" he frantically questioned.

"Yes."

"You miss me, don't you?"

"Yes, but..."

"Then this is the best thing for our family. When I'm home you'll see everything will be better."

Foolishly, I fell for his lure hook, line, and sinker. Believing the army was partly responsible for his actions made it easier to hope he would be different. I wrote the letter and mailed it to the commanding officer. Before long, he was discharged from the army. We stayed with my husband's family when he returned to Texas. When we got our first apartment, it filled me with a sense of pride and satisfaction. I really believed that we would be able to make our marriage work.

The apartment itself wasn't anything spectacular. It had two bedrooms, a living area, and a kitchen. Together, we had signed for this place of our own. That made it special. With a new sense of commitment, I forged ahead undaunted by our past experiences. For now, my husband was his old self and I felt renewed.

The next few months went by uneventfully. I was happy and satisfied, but the romance period

The Ministry of Motherhood

of the domestic violence cycle was short lived. When his brother came to our home for a visit during his furlough from the army, the true colors of my husband's rage returned. It was like Déjà vu. When his brother left, my husband accused me of trying to seduce him.

One blow and then another, this altercation was the end of our marriage. I picked up whatever I could find to strike back. I was no match for my husband. I could've gone, but the children were there. He knew I would never leave them. Besides, he would never allow me to.

Finding myself in a life or death situation that night, I knew if I was able to devise a plan to kill him, I was able to carry it out. My children needed their mother and jail was not an option. So, for the last time, I left. He would never lay another hand on me. Nothing I had done could ever justify the type of treatment I was receiving. I would end it once and for all, here and now. If we managed to get through this fight with both of us alive, I would never again live alone with him.

CHAPTER TWELVE

"The Prodigal Daughter"

Luke 15:24 For this son was dead and has now returned to life. He was lost, but now he is found. So the party began.

The story of the prodigal son is all too familiar to many of us. It's the story of a rebellious son that rejected everything he knew, everything he was taught, and chose his own way. Prideful and headstrong, the son takes his inheritance, leaves his father, and travels to a far land. Squandering everything he had on a lavish lifestyle, the son soon returns home contrite in spirit. Recognizing failure and despair, the son repents and is willing to do anything to win back his father's approval. Surprisingly, the father welcomes his son home with open arms. He even throws a party. The father's unconditional love for his son knew no bounds.

Demonstrating God the Father's unconditional love for his children, this parable shows God's compassion, grace, patience, and willingness to welcome each of us home when we go astray. Faith and forgiveness flourish as the "Prodigal Son" returns home.

Motherhood Ministers emulate these traits when dealing with their children. My mother had a PhD in this area.

I was the prodigal daughter. I strayed away from the teachings that had kept from harm all of my life. I thought I had everything worked out. If not for the prayers of my mother, my life would have been much worse. The covering that she placed on my life still exists with me today.

Having been right all along did not stop my mother from welcoming me with open arms. Much like God, she allowed me to make my choices, good or bad. When the bad ones knocked me down, she was always there to pick me up, dust me off, and help me move forward.

My mother was always my biggest fan. She supported me emotionally, financially, physically, and spiritually. Because of her, I was able to accomplish much more that I ever could have alone.

Even though I rebelled against her and turned against her teachings, she still took me in. Unconditional love was always her banner,

The Ministry of Motherhood

and she waived it proudly whenever one of her children needed to see it.

CHAPTER THIRTEEN

"Tried by the Fire"

Isaiah 43:2 When you pass through the waters, I will be with you; and through the rivers, they shall not overflow you. When you walk through the fire, you shall not be burned, nor shall the flame scorch you.

There's reference in Proverbs 31 that likens women to rubies. Learning rubies are made valuable by going through fire, I understand why Solomon made the reference. When you play with fire, you're going to get burned, but God was with me and I was neither burned nor scorched.

Companionship with anyone else had never crossed my mind since the relationship with my husband had been going on since the ninth grade. But, getting back in the game was necessary and my friends agreed. While I had never really been the kind of girl to pursue men, I decided if someone was interested, I would at least give them a chance. This wasn't easy though. I had a lot of baggage to deal with. If a man even looked at me the wrong way, I was ready to pounce on him like a lion. I had to maintain control of the situation at all costs or I would wind up in another abusive situation.

Concern for my children dictated my every move. Parading a constant flow of men around my boys wasn't an option because I didn't want them to believe relationships were some sort of happenstance occurrence to be taken lightly. Of course, the idea of any companionship for me didn't sit well with my soon to be ex-husband.

One evening after I had been with a male friend, my ex-husband showed up at my parents' doorstep. He claimed that he wanted to talk about the boys. Believing that he wouldn't dare try anything knowing that my parents were in the other room, I let him in.

Shockingly, as we completed our conversation, he suddenly stopped and dropped to his knees. Petrified, I froze into position not knowing what he was going to do next. He pulled me toward him and smelled my crotch. I wanted to scream, but my parents were in the next room and I didn't want to alarm them. So, I just stood there like a statue perched on a pedestal. I thought I would die. Then he said, "I

The Ministry of Motherhood

know you were out with some nigga' tonight, but you better remember that this is mine."

I couldn't believe that he had been following me the entire time! I was terrified. Looking over my shoulder became a way of life after that moment.

CHAPTER FOURTEEN

"Fear Not"

Genesis 21 17-19 17 But God heard the boy crying, and the angel of God called to Hagar from heaven, "Hagar, what's wrong? Do not be afraid! God has heard the boy crying as he lies there. 18 Go to him and comfort him, for I will make a great nation from his descendants." 19 Then God opened Hagar's eyes, and she saw a well full of water. She quickly filled her water container and gave the boy a drink.

Living paycheck to paycheck as a single mom is far too common. Even with the financial support I was receiving from my parents, it was still hard to make ends meet. Money was elusive and difficult to acquire. My public assistance application was turned down because I lived with my parents. Affording an attorney to fight my husband, who wouldn't sign divorce papers, was like pulling teeth. So for now, I was still married.

Low wages, transportation problems, health care costs, and day to day living expenses made it next to impossible to get ahead. Working everyday didn't keep me from being at poverty's door. I was one paycheck away from homelessness. Prideful and strong-willed, I hated to ask my parents for anything. Nevertheless, I swallowed my pride because my children's welfare and quality of life were at stake.

God's providence is so amazing when you're in the situation you don't quite understand. I thought about how cruel the system was. Didn't they know that my children needed to eat just like everyone else? I really needed the assistance, or so I thought.

"Hello, I said. I'm calling to check on my request for assistance with getting child support from my husband. The attorney general's office was never successful, so I thought I'd try your agency."

Somehow, the attorney general is only concerned if you are on public assistance.

"Well, ma'am, I know we promise to get results even when the attorney general'ss office can't, but in your case, everyone is trying to get money from your ex-husband," the person on the other line replied. "We have been unsuccessful in every attempt. I'm sorry."

The Ministry of Motherhood

Something inside me quickened. Angry at the thought that he would get away without having any responsibility for supporting our children, I began to cry. Then, like a breath of fresh air, something spoke to me and said, "Fear not because I am with you always."

More resolved than ever, I picked myself up and decided to accept accountability for my poor choices. It was now my responsibility to see to it my children did not suffer because of my foolishness. God had not given me the spirit of fear, but of love, power, and a sound mind. My love for my children would provide me with the power to succeed. The gifts that God had blessed me with would lead me on a path of sound financial footing for us all.

Not having assistance actually made me a better person. It was a blessing in disguise. It made me work harder for what I wanted out of life. I didn't become a statistic and neither did my boys.

HAGAR

Genesis 21:17-19 "God heard the boy crying and the angel of God called to Hagar from heaven and said to her, "What is the matter Hagar? Do not be afraid. God has heard the boy crying as he lies there. Lift the boy up and take him by the hand for I will make him into a great nation." Then God opened her eyes and she saw a well of water. So she went and filled the skin with water and gave the boy a drink.

Hagar was a slave in a foreign land. She was the maid servant of Abraham's wife, Sarah. When God promised Sarah that she would have a son, Sarah became anxious and told her maidservant to sleep with her husband, Abraham. The result was a son, Ishmael. Sarah became the first surrogate mother.

When God made good on his promise to Sarah, she had a son, Jacob. Sarah became very jealous of Hagar and Ishmael. She had Abraham, her husband, to send Hagar and Ishmael into the desert. Hagar found herself in the wilderness with her son. No water, no food, no money; destitute. Hagar placed Ishmael under a bush when she believed their death was eminent. But, Hagar heard a voice telling her to get her son and take him by the hand because God was going to make a great nation from Ishmael.

God made a way in the wilderness for a single woman and her son; a woman with no friends, no family, and no resources.

Many women today are in "Hagar" situations; disenfranchised, set apart, and alone; living paycheck to paycheck with no end in sight.

I was in the wilderness. Not a literal wilderness, but a wilderness of the mind. Lost, confused, and fearful, I didn't know where to turn. Burdening my family further was the last thing I wanted to do. So, even in the midst of the support, I felt alone.

My children deserve better than me, I lamented over and over again. I never seem to be able to make ends meet. Robbing Peter to pay Paul was getting old. My children shouldn't have to suffer for my poor choices."

Two steps forward, three steps back. When would I see the light at the end of the tunnel? I was tired of the struggle, the heartache, the

The Ministry of Motherhood

disillusionment, the pain. Was God even listening?

Realizing it's at our weakest that God is at His strongest, made sense to me only after I read the most prolific story of struggle I have ever known: The story of Job. Reading this book places one in an attitude of thanksgiving.

Materially, Job lost everything he had; friends, health, wealth, power, everything. Even Job's wife, whom he loved dearly, told Job to curse his God and die. Job was not being punished for any sin that he committed as many of the townspeople believed. In fact, Job was a faithful servant. Allowing the devil to test Job's faith was a testament of God to the faithfulness of Job's service. In the midst of his test, Job trusted God. In return, God gave Job more than he ever had.

We are overcomers by the word of our testimony. If we never experience struggle, if we never deal with the issues of life, then how can we know and trust God's promises to be truth? God never promised us our lives would not have struggles. God's promises are love and protection, no matter what your wilderness experience, poverty, loneliness, or low self esteem. These promises are just as available today as they were for Hagar. You must reach out to God, plan your work, and work your plan. All things work together for the good of those who love the Lord.

A PRAYER FOR FINANCES

Father, it is Your will that Your children live life abundantly. I believe that those persons who seek Your face for a breakthrough in their finances; You will have whatever they need added unto them. Lord, I confess that they will lean on You and not on their own understanding. Remind them that they don't need to climb the mountain. Instead, they should speak to the mountain, in faith, and the mountain will move.

Father, I recognize that the love of money is the root of all kinds of evil. Therefore, I pray that those who read this book will commit to govern their finances in obedience with Your word. You have commanded blessings on their storehouses. I confess that they will become lenders and not borrowers. I declare that they will be good stewards over their financial blessings. Provide them with the resources necessary to effectively care for their children.. I call forth a release of new anointing in the areas of creativity, entrepreneurship, and new businesses.

Father help us to live within our means. Father, I pray for financial increase. Help these readers to love people and use money. I pray for the release of old mindsets and generational curses of poverty and reliance on the system.

Forgive us for patterns of financial failure, patterns of living beyond our means, the overuse of payday loans and pawn shops. Forgive those men and women who have contributed to poverty situations by not paying child support. Forgive us for walking by sight and not by faith. Remind us of those we need to forgive.

Lead us not into temptation, but deliver us from the evil one.

For Yours is the kingdom, and the power, and the glory forever, amen.

CHAPTER FIFTEEN

"The Spirit of Fear"

Deuteronomy 31:6 Be strong and courageous. Do not be afraid or terrified because of them, for the Lord your God goes with you; he will never leave you nor forsake you.

As a single mom, daycare was hard to come by. When the kids were out of school, I had no one to watch them because my mother worked for the school district and many times, she had to go to work even though the children were out. On this particular morning, I found myself in that situation.

The morning started out like any other; sunny, hot, and very humid. Such is the life in the great state of Texas. This particular day though, would be a defining moment in my life. The children didn't have school that day. They were too young to stay home alone and the daycare didn't take children for one day. Taking off from work was not an option. So, I was faced with the difficult task of finding a sitter.

Against my better judgment, I took my children to their father who was living with his parents at the time. I drove the fifteen or so miles to their home with butterflies in my stomach. I couldn't shake the uneasy feeling that I had. Don't let anyone tell you that woman's intuition isn't real. God blesses us with a feeling deep down inside, in our gut, when He is trying to tell us something. Yes, a woman's intuition is very real. I knew something wasn't right, but I had no choice.

I began to rehearse over and over in my mind what I would do when I got there; drop the kids off at the front door, watch them go in, and leave quickly. I didn't want to give their father the opportunity to get near me. I didn't want to be placed in a compromising position.

Initially, everything progressed as planned. But, all of the rehearsal in the world couldn't have prepared me for what was about to happen next.
In my wildest dreams, I never could have imagined that the father of my children could be so calculating, so coldhearted, and so cruel.

I arrived at my in-laws home determined to follow my plan to the letter. I dropped the boys off, still groggy from their sleep. I watched them

The Ministry of Motherhood

step inside. I immediately turned the key in the ignition and started my car.

As I was pulling away, I heard my husband yelling something to me. I stopped, rolled down the window, and asked him what he said.

"Your mother is on the phone," he yelled.

"Why would my mother be calling me?" I thought. "Something must be wrong."

Cell phones were not readily available at this time. I chose to believe him. I put my car in reverse and parked in the driveway.

I proceeded to the front door with apprehension, but I also knew I didn't want to keep my mother waiting.

Once inside the house, I noticed that all of the curtains were drawn and no lights were on. Even in the morning sunlit hours, the house seemed eerily dark.

I moved toward the kitchen quickly. I spotted the phone, but what I saw frightened me. The phone was dangling loosely beside the hard and cold countertop. A busy signal chillingly reverberated throughout the room.

I could feel my stomach touch my back. Fear raced over me like a stampede of horses trying desperately to cross the finish line at the Kentucky Derby. My heart was ticking like a time bomb that would go off at any minute. My head was pounding so hard I thought it would explode. My brain was telling my feet to run, but they didn't move fast enough. By the time I made it back to the front door, it was locked and my worst nightmare was about to come true.

It was like a scene from a horror movie. All of a sudden, I felt like I was in a tunnel and the closer I moved toward the door, the further away it seemed.

I tried to move his five foot eight frame away from the door, but my five foot three inches was simply no match for him. My frantic attempts were useless.

Slowly, he inched toward me like a snake about to devour his prey. My mind drew a complete blank as panic set in. I tried furiously to figure out an escape route.

As often as I had been in this house, it never dawned on me there was only one way in and one way out.

Frantically, I tried to run away, but to no avail. He grabbed me and drew me near to him, pulling me into his chest, forcing me to witness, at face value, the disgusting person he had become. I quietly begged and pleaded for him to let me go, for the sake of our children. I implored, "Please," hoping that the love he claimed he still had for me would allow him to be merciful. My pleas fell on deaf ears as he was more than determined to have his way, to make me pay for rejecting him. Nothing made sense anymore, at that moment, all was blurry and unclear to me.

I knew that my children would be frightened and confused about the mayhem that was taking place, so, in the spirit of motherhood and for the protection of my children at any cost, I closed my eyes, braced myself, and became silent and still. In my mind, I tried to take myself to another place, perhaps putting a wall up and God's armor on, because I wanted to be as far away from there as possible.

My heart raced so fast as the panic set in. Just to think the man I had fallen in love with, given my heart and soul to, defiled me in such a manner, that it was hard to comprehend. All I could think of was when the madness would be over. And through the midst of the storm, I managed to pray, begged God to shield this evil from my children.

My children were my main concern. They were the only reason that I could withstand what was happening to me. I couldn't bear the thought of them being harmed in any way so, I kept quiet and motionless.

I'm sure that my husband thought he had won. The truth is, the depth of a mother's love sometimes goes so deep that even the most tragic of situations can cause her to triumph over adversity for her children's sake.

After the torment was over, I quietly and quickly gathered the children as my husband looked on with a smile of satisfaction on his face. Some sort of twisted victory, a sick euphoria glazed over his face, and convinced me that he had not only lost his mind, he also lost his soul. I got back into my vehicle, thankful that at the very least, God spared my life. Lord knows I needed to be here with and for my children. We drove away silently and I was in a daze.

Disheveled, heartbroken, and disillusioned, I called my mother at work.

"Mama?" I cried.

"Yes, Cheryl, what's wrong?" As a minister of motherhood, my mother immediately knew something was wrong.

"Something bad happened, Mama," I expelled between sniffles and tears. "Something really bad, please come home."

"What happened, Cheryl?" she yelled and questioned frantically.

"Mom, just come home, please," I muffled, barely able to get the sentence from my mind to my tongue.

"Cheryl!" she screamed.

I hung up the phone.

A friend of mine, concerned that I had not shown up for work, called me. When I told her what had happened, she too rushed to be by my side.

Within the hour, both my Mother and my friend were at the house. As my Mother approached me, I lowered my head in shame. Her strong hands grabbed me by my face and demanded I tell her what happened to me. Her tear-filled eyes scanned me from top to bottom, and with each stare, she became more saddened.

 Sadness consumed me and I began to feel weak. As tears flooded my eyes and poured profusely from my face, I lifted my head, and with despair, I stared back at my Mother and revealed to her the suffering I endured at the hands of her son-in-law.

"I dropped the children off. And..."

"And, what, Cheryl?" she demanded.

"He said you were on the phone..."

The Ministry of Motherhood

"I would never call you there. Oh God, what happened, Cheryl? What did he do to you!" she yelled a loud and thunderous moan.
I felt her soul aching.
She tried to walk away to gain her balance, but my revelation knocked the wind out of her. As she leaned on the arm of the sofa to regain her composure, I rushed over to help her. It was at this time that God gave both of us strength. As I tried to help her, she wrapped her arms around me, pulled me close to her, and vowed that we'd get through it all.
"I'm so sorry, baby. I can't believe this. I can't believe that bastard hurt my baby again. We're gonna get through this."
Together, we called the police to report the incident.
"Houston Police Department, how may I direct your call?" the voice on the other side of the phone inquired.
"I want to report an incident," I said..
"What kind of incident ma'am?"
"An assault," I replied.
"One moment please."

The next few moments were almost surreal. Minutes felt like hours, until someone picked up the phone and I began explaining exactly what happened to me at the hands of my husband.
Then, I received a reply that I didn't anticipate. It took the wind out of my already fragile sails.
"I'm sorry, ma'am, but there's nothing we can do. This is classified as a domestic dispute. We can file a complaint, but that's as far as it will go."

"What?" I questioned, full of rage. You mean to tell me that nothing can be done after all of the pain he's put me through. He just gets away with it?"

After being humiliated and violated once again, I threw the phone down with intense anger and vengeance, and sobbed uncontrollably. The heartache and pain I felt became so overwhelming. Immediately, my mother picked up the phone, said goodbye, and tried unsuccessfully to console me.

After bearing my very soul to this female officer, hoping that I would receive some kind of compassion, all she could offer me was a complaint filed with the department. Why was the system this way? How could they just let someone get away with an act as heinous as this? It's just not right! It's not fair! These were the first thoughts that I had after I came out of my fog.

Disappointed and inconsolable, I cleaned myself up, changed clothes, and never spoke of this incident again until now. No one, except someone who has been through this before, could possibly understand how much this entire ordeal hurts. It is a violation, not only physically, it also tears at the very fabric and foundation of a woman's life. It can change everything. It can slowly devour your soul and demolish your spirit if you let it.

It was at this time that my foundation, rooted in the word of God, had been shattered. I was trying to do right, yet, I was being knocked down at every turn, now this? For a split-

The Ministry of Motherhood

second, I questioned God, His motives, and His powers.

After this, how was I ever to trust another man again? How would I ever be able to have intimate feelings again? How could I trust even my own judgment? The destructive actions of abuse and its messages threatened to bind me. The guilt and shame that I felt engulfed me like a flame. I struggled not to internalize the destructive messages so that I wouldn't end up in a place that God didn't intend for my life. Internalizing the violence caused self blame, rather than the ability to see myself in the process of becoming.

You see, you struggle everyday to hold on to a little piece of your soul so that it doesn't end up slipping away completely. My children were a large part of that.

God, through the love of my children, convinced me to leave my troubles with Him. That moment that I questioned God, was traded for a lifetime of devotion to Him.

It may sound strange now, but I thank God everyday for my ex-husband (he became my ex-husband many years later when I filed my divorce myself) because he taught me many things. Not the kind of lessons you can learn in a classroom or in Sunday school, but lessons that can only come from experience, wisdom, and maturity.

Without him, I may never have learned how resilient I could truly be. I would not know the true meaning of forgiveness.

How does one come back from such trauma and forgive? It isn't easy, but I heard someone say that being unable to forgive is like drinking poison and expecting someone else to die. Not forgiving only hurts you. Usually, the perpetrator has long since moved on. You, the victim, are left to become bitter, vengeful, and resentful. If you're not careful, you'll find yourself all alone as people slowly move away because of your constant inability to maintain healthy relationships.

Consciously deciding to forgive my ex-husband for the atrocities committed against me, left some people wondering if I had lost my mind. Even now, some people don't understand it. Not realizing that had I not chosen to forgive my life would be on a downward spiral, many people still question my judgment, even now.

Let me make it clear, I didn't forget what my husband did to me, nor did I deny his responsibility. I simply chose to untie myself from the thoughts and feelings that bound me to my ex-husband's offenses. Refusing to minimize what had been done to me, I gave the hurt, shame, disappointment, and humiliation to God and I allowed the Holy Spirit to help me forgive my ex-husband and myself.

Forgiving him enriched my life in ways that no one could ever imagine.

Learning to release all of the guilt, anger, bitterness, resentment, revenge and fear to God before I moved on allowed me to let go of the past so that I wouldn't continue to live in it. I

The Ministry of Motherhood

moved into my future. And what a brilliant future it has been.

Being able to recognize the kind of man I didn't want in my life was the most important lesson that my ex-husband taught me.

Through the fire and the rain, through the joy and the pain, I thank God for the wisdom I gained.

TAMAR

2 Samuel 13:12 "Don't my brother!" she said to him. "Don't force me. Such a thing should not be done in Israel! Don't do this wicked thing. What about me? Where could I get rid of my disgrace? And what about you? You would be like one of the wicked fools in Israel. Please speak to the king. He will not keep me from being married to you." But he refused to listen to her and since he was stronger that she, he raped her.

Violent, brutal, and degrading flashbacks of sounds, sights, and smells can trigger old memories of rape and sexual abuse. Considering suicide or homicide is the price that will be paid emotionally after such a soul crushing ordeal. Surprising some, but known to others, the Bible illustrates the horrors of sexual abuse in stories told throughout its pages.

Tamar was the daughter of King David. The Bible says that she was beautiful just like her father. Her destiny was to become married to someone who could improve her father's political alliances.

Tamar, nor her father, knew that the future they had planned would soon be destroyed.
Amnon, Tamar's half brother and the heir to the throne was in love with Tamar. Amnon's love led him to carry out an unspeakable act on his sister. He raped her.

Samuel 2:13 describes Tamar's impassioned pleas to her brother. She begged him not to defile her virginity. Amnon, being stronger than Tamar, forced himself on her. Tamar had no effective means of resistance.

To add insult to injury, David, the father of both Tamar and Amnon, did nothing to punish Amnon.

Losing her virginity forced Tamar to live with her brother, Absalom, with no possibility of becoming a "real woman"; no marriage, no children.
Punished in the end, Amnon was killed by his half brother, Absalom.

Haunting a woman forever, the effects of such an event can influence her relationships with everyone she comes in contact with, including her children. Comforting the victim with clichés like, "take your burdens to the Lord and leave them there." Or, "what doesn't kill you makes you stronger "are commendable

The Ministry of Motherhood

efforts, but what you really need is a breakthrough.

Reacting disdainfully to sexual sin, God's word reflects His thoughts on the subject.

It's important to note that God not only offers comfort to the victim, He also offers healing and forgiveness to the perpetrator.

God doesn't turn away from the victim and he doesn't allow the person responsible to go unpunished.

Allowing God to bring healing and comfort that soothed the hurts of the past, and delivering me from the hold of the past while he bound my wounds and restored my soul, is how I experienced my breakthrough.

Renewing my way of thinking about the situation and understanding that I was more than a conqueror and an over-comer by the word of my testimony, helped me to release myself from the guilt and the anger. Letting go of the past, refusing to live in it, and learning from it deepened my relationship with God.

Immersing yourself in the revelation of God's word, you rediscover His love and acceptance. You recapture the sense of security that was destroyed when you were violated by the perpetrator.

Only by His Word and His grace am I able to write these words today. For many years, this terrible act had been buried deep in the recesses of my heart. God has set me free and I am forever grateful.

A PRAYER TO FORGIVE OTHERS

Lord, You are the Alpha and the Omega, the beginning and the end. You are the God who is, and was, and is to come. We are in awe of Your great works for they are marvelous in our eyes. Today, we bow down and worship You.

God, Your word tells us that if we forgive those who have harmed us, You will forgive us. Father, I ask You to help those that read this book to forgive. Heal their emotions, bind their wounds, restore their souls, and instruct them how to love unconditionally. Enable them to not carry grudges or hold things in their hearts. I confess that they will no longer be blinded by the darkness of un-forgiveness. Enable them to love their enemies, bless those who curse them, do good to those who hate them, and pray for those who spitefully use them. Pour forgiveness into their hearts so that bitterness, resentment, and revenge will have no place there. Holy Spirit help them to use the power within them to love and forgive. Remind them that vengeance is Yours, O God.

Forgive them for not forgiving. Forgive them for thinking evil thoughts and thoughts of seeking revenge. Forgive them for hatred and for not walking in love. Help them to forgive.

Lead them not into temptation, but deliver them from the evil one. For Yours in the kingdom, and the power, and the glory, forever, Amen.

My Testimony...

CHAPTER SIXTEEN

"Claiming My Reward"

Psalms 127:3 Children are a gift from the LORD; they are a reward from him.

Children are a gift from God. Unlike the gifts we receive at Christmas, we cannot wrap them up and take them back when we are not satisfied with the product. Because such a high price was paid for their delivery, we can't push them to the side like a pair of old shoes. Being a mother is not a task for the faint at heart. To be successful, it takes a lot of time and effort, particularly if you have to be both mother and father to your children.

Sports was never something that I really enjoyed. Even though I attended many games when I was in school, it was because of the clubs and organizations with which I was affiliated. Having boys changed all that.

I tried to learn everything that I could about football, basketball, and baseball so that I could intelligently attend games in which my boys were playing.

These were the kinds of things that should've been reserved for their father, but he wasn't around.

I often wondered if my children would suffer because their father wasn't in their lives. Would they long to get to know him better? Would they long for more than the haphazard meetings they had from time to time at the grandparents' home? Would they miss having someone to call Daddy? Would they struggle to know their existence, value, worth, or purpose? Would they miss their father teaching them how to ride a bike, or throw a football?

Hatred for my ex consumed me most completely at these moments. Not for myself, but for my children. They didn't deserve this. No matter how he felt about me, they were still his children. Walking away from them was his choice. He never considered the impact his absence would have on their lives.

To punish me, he left me and my family to foot the bill. He even bragged about it. He would call my mother and say things like, " I don't do anything because I know you have it taken care of." By the grace of God, we survived.

The Ministry of Motherhood

I gradually developed an affinity for many sports. In my ex's absence, I was determined not to let them miss out.

Little league was an experience all its own. You must pay for everything if you want your children to participate. Many times, I would forgo paying certain bills so they could enjoy the fun and camaraderie that sports had to offer.

When the lights or water were cut off, I managed to find a way to get them back on. On many occasions, that way was my parents. I hated going to them, but it was my only choice.

The attorney general's office didn't seem to care that my husband wasn't paying his court ordered child support since I wasn't on welfare. So, getting any help from him was out of the question. Funny, somehow receiving child support from my ex ceased to matter. I comforted myself in knowing that the boys wouldn't have to visit him and be subjected to his tirades. There were many times that I would pay the electric bill with a check written to the gas company and vice versa. This would buy me some time until I got paid again. The bottom line was, my sons would succeed no matter what I had to do, or what sacrifices I had to make.

As my children grew older, they participated in school sports. This was both a blessing and a curse. Some evenings, I would be so tired I couldn't see straight, but I was determined that my children would see my face in the crowd. I would be the one that they heard cheering the loudest whenever their name was called. I was a team mom for just about every sport imaginable. They could always count on me. It wasn't unusual for me to come home to find an entire football team waiting to see "what's for dinner." I loved it, mostly because I always knew where my children were.

Sports was not the only area in which I made my presence known. School was probably the single most important part of our lives. An education would be the ticket to a successful future. It was a must for African American males in this country. My boys were no exception. As long as they were in school, I participated in the PTA, volunteered to be the room mother, and showed up for school conferences.

One such conference happened as a result of my youngest son's behavior in class. It seemed that he suffered from the same problem that I did in school. He would finish his work ahead of time and then visit with everyone else in class.
When I arrived on the campus, the principal was shocked to see me. I don't know if it was because I made it there in thirty minutes or if it was because I came for such a minor offense. In either case, he was glad to see me. He confided in me that most parents, the ones who really needed to be there, rarely showed up. I made it clear to the principal and the teacher that my sons and I were on a mission. They were there simply to absorb what the teachers had to offer, not to be disruptive in class.

This was not my first visit to the school, nor would it be my last. I frequently made surprise visits to ensure accountability on the part of my

The Ministry of Motherhood

children as well as the instructor. I wanted to make sure they received the kind of education they deserved.

Their instruction did not begin and end in the classroom either. I rarely waited on the school to teach them anything. I took my boys on educational outings every chance I got. It was reinforcement for what they were being taught in class. I became well informed about every free event in the Houston area. On a regular basis, I would take the boys to the museum to see various exhibits that had come to town. Of course, the Museum of Natural Science was a hit because of the dinosaur display. I also found other ways to spend quality time with my children. We must've eaten at every kids eat free establishment in the city. Of course, the kids didn't care that it was free. All they knew was that we were out on the town and having a good time.

Money is not what children need. Love, attention, and quality time, that's what makes successful children. They shouldn't have to wait for the world to validate them. To this day, you can't convince my children that we were one paycheck from poverty everyday. Not because they got everything they wanted, but because they got everything they needed; time, attention, love, and a solid foundation.

PATIENCE IS A VIRTUE

Job 39:14-16 *She leaves her eggs in the earth to be warmed in the dust and forgets that the foot may crush them or that the wild beast may break them. She is hardened against her young even as though they were not hers.*

When during the process of raising your children you find yourself lost and struggling, remember, your children count on you to keep their world safe and happy. Your children are your greatest legacy and you are their greatest protector. God has bestowed you with the heavy responsibility of nurturing another person's soul. Don't take that responsibility lightly.

I know sometimes it feels like you're a hamster in a cage, just spinning your wheels, running frantically, 100 miles an hour to nowhere, but believe me, it's worth it. As mothers, we must keep a right attitude about our family. Giving birth to a child doesn't mean she is transformed from a woman into a mother overnight. Giving birth simply means God has granted you the gift of producing life. The real challenge comes when after having birthed that child, you dedicate your life, wholeheartedly, to raising that child. Unfortunately, there are those who remain selfish and heartless until they die.

Accusing the mother's in his day of cruelty and neglect, Jeremiah causes us to reflect on the mothers of our day. Child abuse, molestation, gangs, and drugs; these problems are an outcome of selfish, neglectful mothers, mothers that think only of themselves and their needs. These mothers are too busy having a good time to be worried about taking care of their own children.

In Isaiah 3:16-26, Isaiah articulates Gods feelings about women pursuing the wrong goals and their outcome.

The LORD says, "The women of Zion are haughty, walking along with outstretched necks, flirting with their eyes, tripping along with mincing steps, with ornaments jingling on their ankles. Therefore the Lord will bring sores on the heads of the women of Zion; the LORD will make their scalps bald." In that day the Lord will snatch away their finery: the bangles and headbands and crescent necklaces, the earrings and bracelets and veils, 20 the headdresses and ankle chains and sashes, the

The Ministry of Motherhood

perfume bottles and charms, the signet rings and nose rings, the fine robes and the capes and cloaks, the purse, and mirrors, and the linen garments and tiaras and shawls. Instead of fragrance there will be a stench; instead of a sash, a rope; instead of well-dressed hair, baldness; instead of fine clothing, sackcloth; instead of beauty, branding. Your men will fall by the sword, your warriors in battle. The gates of Zion will lament and mourn; destitute, she will sit on the ground.

Dressing to gain approval and be noticed, these women focused more on their appearance than they focused on God. Self serving, self centered, neglecting the oppression all around them, these women turned away from God's purpose in their lives. Using people and loving things only results in your being bankrupt, materially and spiritually.

These scriptures remind us of the women of our day. It's no wonder that our children are so lost.

Train up a child in the way he should go and when he is old he will not depart from it
Proverbs 22:6

This is the Bible's commission to parents. But, what does training really mean? Leading your children by faith to Christ and being a consistent example to them is the first step in training. Difficult but effective, leading by example communicates our commitment to live out the truth and reality of Jesus in our lives. Defined more by what we don't do than what we do as mothers, we must be diligent in our prayer life, in our church going, and in the way we interact with people on a daily basis. Knowing Christian doctrine, using Christian vernacular, and appearing Godly may fool outsiders, but it won't fool your children and it won't fool God. Seeing you as you really are, children are in the best position to be students of your life. Having the most insight into the relationship between what you say and what you do, children become the best at deciphering hypocrisy from true Christian discipleship. Gossiping, lying to the bill collector, and constantly bashing our children's father are all poor examples of our faith walk with God. In fact, the very message that these attributes send is one of hypocrisy.

Picking and choosing our sins; I don't smoke, I don't drink, I don't cuss, is more about us than it is about being Christ like. Memorizing scripture is good, but a personal relationship with God is the ultimate goal. Morality is not the only gauge by which we are measured. The cemetery is full of people that didn't do bad things. The question is, was their walk with God close enough to enter the kingdom of heaven? We have all sinned and fallen short of the glory of God.

We can't make Christ a reality to our children if He is not a reality to us. Practice what you want them to practice. Children follow and imitate us. "Do as I say not as I do" is a poor motto to follow if you want to raise Godly children. Remember to teach them by example. Your example. Learning not brought about by both example and instruction will lead to a child that does not respect the parents. Living out the

The Ministry of Motherhood

Christian life through the Holy Spirit will be instruction to your children that Christ is real. Are you creating a desire for God in your children?

Honor must be restored to the institution of motherhood. *"Honor your father and your mother, so that you may live long in the land the LORD your God is giving you. Exodus 20:12.* The Bible clearly illustrates honoring one's parents is pleasing and ordained by God. In fact, this commandment is the first with a promise. *"Honor your father and mother," which is the first commandment with promise: Ephesians 6:2.* Honoring a parent, however, is more easily done when the parent is honorable. Dictating the atmosphere of the home is a mother's responsibility. Walkin' it out in the club harder than your daughter does not bring you honor. Instead, it only demonstrates your willingness to be governed by the world's standards. Whether or not a home is a refuge or a battleground depends solely on the mother's ability to manage the home well. Absent this influence, the child is destined to succumb to the world's lies, fear, and deception.

Romans 1:28-32 gives a grim view of what this looks like. *Furthermore, since they did not think it worthwhile to retain the knowledge of God, he gave them over to a depraved mind; to do what ought not to be done. They have become filled with every kind of wickedness, evil, greed and depravity. They are full of envy, murder, strife, deceit and malice. They are gossips, 0slanderers, God-haters, insolent, arrogant, and boastful; they invent ways of doing evil; they disobey their parents; they are senseless, faithless, heartless, ruthless. Although they know God's righteous decree that those who do such things deserve death, they not only continue to do these very things but also approve of those who practice them.* 2 Timothy *3:2* also paints a negative picture. *People will be lovers of themselves, lovers of money, boastful, proud, abusive, disobedient to their parents, ungrateful, unholy.*

Admonishing us not to provoke our children to anger the Bible suggests we must get to know our children and have a good relationship with them. Look at David, who is the epitome of a father who was disinterested in, and made mistakes with, his children. (2 Samuel 13-18) The end result was an all out war between him and his son. David's adultery, philandering, and eventual arrangement of the murder of Uriah caused Absalom, David's son, to harden his heart toward David. David had provoked his son to anger.

Delicately balancing challenging them to do better without demeaning them, eliminates the threat of provocation. Knowing your children and loving them unconditionally is extremely important. However, in today's society, long work schedules, selfish entertainment choices, and television can totally derail any attempt at a meaningful relationship.

We must challenge our children to succeed. Love your children for who they are, just as they are. Contrary to popular opinion, you cannot

The Ministry of Motherhood

treat all of your children the same. Why? Because they are individuals with different personalities, different temperaments, and different needs. Address each of them according to their individual abilities, and help them to understand their importance as an individual. Giving your children a sense of security and letting them know that they are protected and a part of the family unit will keep them from seeking these assurances elsewhere. Don't ignore or try to explain away fears. Acknowledge them, admit them, and encourage them. Letting children know that you too are afraid, sometimes will allow them the freedom to meet their fears head on and be liberated in God rather than bound by the chains of men's expectations. Understanding the difference between discipline and punishment will allow you to more effectively develop responsible behavior in your child while communicating to them that you care.

Punishments are given as a penalty for an offense. It is usually handed out in hostility and frustration, and produces fear and guilt. Discipline, on the other hand, is used to train and to correct. Discipline must be fair. It needs to be explained to and understood by the child if it is to be effective. Discipline must also be prompt, and delivered as soon after the offense as possible. Finally, discipline must be terminal; no continued reminders, assured reacceptance. In an environment of discipline, the child will learn life's requirements in the context of love and concern. In an environment of true discipline, the child understands the importance of these requirements for their future, for God, and for society.

Reminding ourselves frequently that our children are bound to make the same mistakes we did when we were young helps us to discard hypocritical ideas. Willingness to accept our children will fall short sometimes, and being tolerant of failure moves us toward acceptance which will keep us from giving up on them or tearing them down.

A soft word can turn away wrath, but a harsh word stirs up anger. (Proverbs 15:1)

Patience is a virtue. Reminding ourselves that our heavenly Father still loves us in spite of our failures will help us to think twice before shouting at our children so harshly for their mistakes.

Reasonable, understandable discipline and parents whose own behavior is consistent with the demands placed on the child, will lead to a parent child relationship of mutual love and respect.

A PRAYER FOR SINGLE MOTHERS

Father, You are great and You do wondrous things. Your majestic name fills the earth. You are worthy of all our praise. Hallowed be Your name, Lord.

Father, it is Your will that families prosper and be in good health even as their souls do prosper. I pray that mothers will inspire their children to honor them so that their days may be long upon the earth. I declare that single parents will have peaceful, safe, and quiet homes. I declare that stability, salvation, love, wisdom, and knowledge will encompass their homes. I come against all soul ties, strongholds, and generational curses in their blood lines. I declare that single mothers will be interested, affectionate, involved, strong, consistent, dependable, communicative, understanding, and patient.

Lord, where there is discord in their families, please turn us back to one another. Help these single mothers to be the parents You called them to be. Lord, strengthen and impart Your wisdom into the lives of thee mothers. Help them to model a life that is pleasing to You. Enable them to let go of past mistakes that they may have made with their children. I declare that they will put off former conduct and customary ways of thinking about it. They will be renewed in their minds. I confess that they will grow to understand that if any man be in Christ, he is a new creature. Holy Spirit, show them a fresh way of looking at negative things that happen.

For those desiring a mate, help them to be anxious for nothing and wait on you.

Father, forgive single mothers for sin and all acts of sinfulness, including, abuse, neglect, unkindness, fear, financial mismanagement, and poor parenting. Lord, remind them to forgive others.

Lead them not into temptation, but deliver them from the evil one.

For Yours is the kingdom, and the power, and the glory forever, Amen.

CHAPTER SEVENTEEN

"Second Time Around"

Isaiah 58:8 Your light shall break forth like the morning, your healing shall spring forth speedily, and your righteousness shall go before you; the glory of the Lord shall be your read guard.

After being a single mom for nine years, I finally married again. It was cathartic to say the least. Even now I find myself doing away with baggage from the past. It's not easy, but I am a work in progress. Sharing me the way I wanted to share with the new love of my life was difficult. No one understands what that's like. Waiting to let yourself feel free enough to share intimacy with someone you love so much, but not being able to. You project your negative feelings onto the one person you trust with your life.

The first few years of our marriage were the rockiest. It was more my fault than his. He had to endure my hang-ups. I loved my husband more than anything, but I couldn't allow love to cause me to slip up again.

Giving up control was a problem. I wanted things to be my way or the highway. I was stubborn, dogmatic, and vindictive. Having to be open about my faults made me insecure. I pulled out all the stops to make sure that things were done the way I wanted them done. As long as the ends justified the means, I believed it was okay. I didn't think about what my husband wanted or needed. I couldn't. That would mean that I was weak. Weakness was not an option. Losing control meant losing me. Wanting never again to be in that position, I became tough, determined not to give in, unrelenting in my pursuits, and difficult to sway. Control, however, was elusive. What I had built was a facade, a fake image hiding the scared, intimidated, little girl inside. She was protected by this strong, confident, independent woman who took no prisoners. Her walls were stronger than the one in Berlin. It would take more than freedom to bring them down. Allowing someone to penetrate those walls meant becoming vulnerable, open, and transparent. I wasn't ready. I wanted to remain in a place where I could lash out and have a pity party while identifying everyone else's faults.

The Ministry of Motherhood

I knew my husband loved me, but was it truly unconditional? Should I risk exposing what was inside? If I shared with him what was really inside would he understand? Or, would he take advantage of the fear and insecurity I internalized. Risking the loss of someone I loved dearly by being totally honest was not an option. No, this façade would have to stand for now. A meltdown at this point would leave me spiraling out of control. My children needed me too much. I chose to be content with the pain that placed a lock on my heart and my mind. For now, only I would hold the key.

Understanding why I didn't trust him with my children was a difficult pill for my husband to swallow. But, he managed to move forward in spite of the disappointment. You see, when it came to the boys, they had already been hurt enough by one father. I wasn't going to allow them to be hurt by another.

Besides, my husband was not their biological father and as crazy as it sounds, I didn't want him to be burdened with the mundane tasks of parenting. I know when he married me he knew he was taking on the whole package, but I wanted to be fair. I ran myself ragged trying to go it alone. No matter, the control was mine and I took full responsibility.

Trust was another huge issue for me. I had a problem trusting my own judgment. Trusting someone else with the lives of me and my children was out of the question. For my husband, this translated into endless arguments about his nights out with the fellas. He didn't have them often, but when he did, there was hell to pay. I don't know how he managed to tolerate it, but I thank God that he did.

The most important thing was my husband and I loved each other very much and we were determined to stick it out. I had found my Boaz and I needed to become more like Ruth.

There were times in our marriage when I literally kept divorce papers in the file cabinet. I believed finding a man that could love me unconditionally was too good to be true. I was wrong. We both had a lot of growing up to do. We also had to reconcile the experiences we brought from our families of origin. We had to forge a life that worked for us and not our families.

When we turned our marriage over to God and allowed Him to order our steps according to His plan, our marriage changed for the better. Sharing openly about our relationship with God brought depth to our marriage. Having God as our greatest bond forged a strong, mutual commitment in which each of us has tried to do what we thought was best for the other. Throughout the tough times, we continued to trust God and in His time he blessed us greatly. Even in times of great discord, God brought great blessings.

We stopped relying on outside influences and turned to the word for direction. I stopped trying to change my husband. I did away with my unrealistic expectations for him as well as for myself. I also put away my know-it-all mentality

The Ministry of Motherhood

and realized only God is omniscient. I still work on this daily

My faith has always carried me. I decided to let go and let God. He did. During the toughest times, I'd sit and talk to God. I'd tell Him about my dreams. I'd talk about feeling as if nothing was going right in my life. I'd tell Him about not wanting to go to my parents for money anymore. I was always stronger after these moments. In my weakest moment, God was my pillar of strength.

RUTH AND BOAZ

*Ruth 2:10: Why have I found such favor in
your eyes that you notice me?*

Occurring during a period of disobedience and violence, the story of Ruth and Boaz indicates to us that even in times of crises and deep despair, there are those people who still follow God. As a result, He uses them to achieve His purpose.

Ruth was a poor widow. After joining God's people, she risks her honor at the feet of Boaz. Ruth eventually becomes Boaz's wife. Ruth's beginnings help us to understand how we can start out with no hope as rebellious foreigners, only to risk everything by putting our faith in God and being given blessings that will last forever.

Boaz was a rich man, yet, he was wise enough to respect and admire the courage, devotion, kindness, and fidelity of Ruth. Like many of us, Ruth felt her past made her less than any other woman. Boaz demolished this misconception and acknowledged her with honor. Knowing that Ruth was more than the culmination of her past issues and present circumstances, Boaz understood and revered Ruth. He honored the woman she was within and the woman she could become if he became her coverer.

For those whose lives are in shambles, this story reminds us of God's love and redeeming power. Ruth obtained favor from an honorable man who loved her and willfully provided, protected, covered, and prayed for her. Boaz loved Ruth because of her character and her heart.

Dealing with devastating circumstances caused me to lose hope in God, but I didn't lose sight of the fact that God's resources are never ending. Believing that He could work in my life strengthened my trust in His protection. I now know that I was blessed with a Boaz. God's very best. Thinking of this blessing not in terms of prosperity, but in terms of the relationship God so graciously provided for me, helped me to clear my clouded judgment. Loving and respecting the person that God had placed in my life opened me up to give and receive blessings that are immeasurable. Being able to overcome the differences that might have led to division

The Ministry of Motherhood

allowed us to experience God's living presence in our relationship.

Submitting to God allowed me to find the one He had for me. Waiting for His timing in my life allowed me to encounter a love that seemed elusive.

When you feel as though your poor choices have taken you away from God's plan for your life, remember God's redeeming power. Repent and go back to Him. Be encouraged. God's promises are yes and amen. The Holy Spirit is here to work with you.

HAPPILY EVER AFTER AGAIN

1 Peter 5:7 Cast all your anxiety on him because he cares for you.

Cultivating your marriage is necessary in three areas: commitment, conflict management, and communication. Misalignment in any of these areas can lead to failure. Relationships, rather than roles and rules, is what's really important. Listening, understanding, and desiring to understand are essential.

If you haven't made a commitment to pray daily for your husband, do so today. Surrender your marriage to God. Cast the cares of your marriage on God. Carrying the worries, stresses, and daily struggles of marriage by yourself shows that you have not trusted God fully with all areas of your life. Sometimes, we think that the struggles caused by our own foolish choices are not God's concern. But, when we turn to God in repentance, He will bear the weight of even those struggles. Don't submit to marital strife, but to the Lord who is the head of your marriage. Specifically, ask God to bless your spouse. Stop focusing on your list of complaints and unrealistic expectations. Tearing your husband down verbally and getting back at him when you're hurt is not the answer. In 1 Peter 3:9-12, which says, *Do not repay evil with evil or insult with insult, but with blessing, because to this you were called so that you may inherit a blessing. For, "Whoever would love life and see good days must keep his tongue from evil and his lips from deceitful speech. He must turn from evil and do good; he must seek peace and pursue it. For the eyes of the Lord are on the righteous and his ears are attentive to their prayer, but the face of the Lord is against those who do evil."* Peter reminds us that insulting someone, no matter how indirectly, is unacceptable. Being quarrelsome, naggy, and giving a steady stream of unwanted advice is a form of torture. Several passages in the Bible remind us that a quarrelsome wife is like a constant dripping. Proverbs 19:13; 21:9, 21:19, 27:15. Nagging hinders communication more than it helps. When tempted to engage in this behavior with your husband, stop and examine your motives. Are you more concerned about getting your way? If you are truly concerned about your husband, think of a more effective

The Ministry of Motherhood

way to get through to him. Surprise him with words of patience and love. Pray for your husband's needs. Ask God to use your marriage for his purpose. Where love has died, ask God to create a new love between you. Relinquish any desire you have to control your husband and ask God to work in his life. Resign as you husband's mother. You married an adult. Treat your husband with the respect that he deserves.

While you're asking, ask God to also work on you. *James 3:2-18 We all stumble in many ways. If anyone is never at fault in what he says, he is a perfect man, able to keep his whole body in check. When we put bits into the mouths of horses to make them obey us, we can turn the whole animal. Or take ships as an example. Although they are so large and are driven by strong winds, they are steered by a very small rudder wherever the pilot wants to go. Likewise the tongue is a small part of the body, but it makes great boasts. Consider what a great forest is set on fire by a small spark. The tongue also is a fire, a world of evil among the parts of the body. It corrupts the whole person, sets the whole course of his life on fire, and is itself set on fire by hell. All kinds of animals, birds, reptiles and creatures of the sea are being tamed and have been tamed by man, but no man can tame the tongue. It is a restless evil, full of deadly poison. With the tongue we praise our Lord and Father, and with it we curse men, who have been made in God's likeness. Out of the same mouth come praise and cursing. My brothers, this should not be. Can both fresh water and salt water flow from the same spring? My brothers, can a fig tree bear olives, or a grapevine bear figs? Neither can a salt spring produce fresh water. Who is wise and understanding among you? Let him show it by his good life, by deeds done in the humility that comes from wisdom. But if you harbor bitter envy and selfish ambition in your hearts, do not boast about it or deny the truth. Such "wisdom" does not come down from heaven but is earthly, unspiritual, of the devil. For where you have envy and selfish ambition, there you find disorder and every evil practice. But the wisdom that comes from heaven is first of all pure; then peace-loving, considerate, submissive, full of mercy and good fruit, impartial and sincere. Peacemakers who sow in peace raise a harvest of righteousness.*

Controlling your desire to say what you want is important. Thinking before you speak goes a long way. Ask yourself if what you're about to say is necessary. Is it kind? An uncontrolled tongue can do irrevocable harm. Using your tongue, Satan can divide you and your spouse and pit you against one another. Hateful words can spread destruction quickly. Thinking you can apologize later is a fallacy because the scars will still remain. Although it has been said, "Sticks and stones may break my bones but words will never hurt me," the truth is, words are very powerful. When used angrily, spoken words can destroy a relationship that took years to build. Are you tempted to escalate the conflict? Loving words are the seed of peace.

The Ministry of Motherhood

Ask God to relieve you of any baggage that you may be hanging onto that would cause harm to your marriage. Understand that neither of you are perfect, nor that you don't have what it takes to be a good wife. Release your husband from fulfilling you in areas where you should be looking to God. We each have a need to love and be loved; to have a positive self image and a sense of purpose in life. These needs can never be met by someone external from ourselves. Look inside yourself and work on releasing selfishness, impatience, and irritability. Ask God to help you take your emotional baggage, automatic reactions, self preservation, and rude assumptions and turn it into the fruits of the spirit; love, kindness, gentleness, patience, and longsuffering.

Remember, you have the power of life and death in your own tongue. Instead of speaking negatively about your husband, try concentrating on those things that he does well. Lay down your unrealistic expectations at Jesus' feet. Demonstrate the concept of unconditional love, otherwise, you're merely in lust. Put aside your hurt, anger, and disappointment and seek forgiveness, totally and completely.

Recognize that you can't change your husband. Free him to change in ways only God can bring about.

Become your husband's companion, champion, friend, and support. Create a peaceful, restful, and safe place for him to come home to.

~

A PRAYER FOR MARRIAGES

Father, I confess that husbands will love their wives as Christ loves the church. Wives will respect their husbands. I confess that those who read this book will have husbands that are above reproach, self controlled, and calm. They will not be given to violence or greed. They will rule their houses well. Lord, I come against arguing, violence, lies, rebellion, and cruelty in marriages. I confess that marriages will be protected from the influences of alcohol, drugs, gambling, pornography, lust, and obsession. I confess that the love of God will reign supreme in the marriages of the readers of this book. Lord, I declare that married couples will be shielded from selfishness, neglect, and the evil plans and desires of others. May each partner walk in the fruits of the Spirit. May there be no thought of divorce or infidelity. Lord God, protect marriages from anything that would harm or destroy them.

Holy Spirit, empower married couples to be examples of Your grace and mercy. Set couples free from past hurts, memories, and ties from previous relationships. Remove unrealistic expectations. Increase Your love and security in those marriages that are doing well.

Please forgive married couples for acts of sinfulness. Remind them to forgive each other.

Lead them not into temptation, but deliver them from the evil one.

For Yours is the kingdom, and the power, and the glory forever, Amen.

EPILOGUE

2 Corinthians 10: 4-5 For the weapons of our warfare are not carnal but mighty in God for pulling down strongholds, casting down arguments and every high thing that exalts itself against the knowledge of God, bringing every thought into captivity to the obedience of Christ.

"Oh Mary Mack, Mack, Mack;
All dressed in black, black, black;
24 gold buttons, buttons, buttons;
Up and down her back, back, back."

I can still remember hearing the words in my head like it was yesterday. Sweet, melodious tunes from happy children oblivious to the cares of life. Living in a BET, MTV society has taken us to a place far from

Mayberry. Our children are exposed to far more, far sooner than they need to be. Consequently, teen pregnancies are rampant and HIV is infecting people at a younger and younger age, so much so that a diagnosis of syphilis is actually a relief. Our microwave society believes that any and everything goes. Yet, culture also says that it is the parents' responsibility to monitor what their children are exposed to. What happened to the village?

In days gone by, everyone in the community had similar ideas about what should and shouldn't be shared with children according to their ability to process the information. The school, the church, and ultimately the parents provided children with information in much the same manner.

Today, with thousands of television stations, just as many radio stations, and video games that reward you for acts of violence, parents have little, if any, chance of supervising everything to which their children are exposed. In our times, most families begin with pregnancy rather than marriage.

Children are left alone to raise themselves at an alarming rate. They live in poverty, lack access to health care, and are the victims of abuse.

Most children today can't even think about going outside for fear of being shot down in their prime. Where are the mothers, the teachers of compassion, love, and understanding? I'll tell you where they are, in the club dropping it like

The Ministry of Motherhood

it's hot or working two to three jobs trying to make ends meet.

A writer once wrote, "No nation is greater than its mothers, for they are the makers of men." Motherhood is a gift from God and it should be cherished. Motherhood, massacred and mocked, finds too many mothers exercising selfishness with small regard for their children whom they largely ignore. Where is the love and support? Where are "Big Mama," "Nana," and Grandmother, who can help teach and nurture these young mothers; the Titus 2 women? If we don't cure the disease that is eating away at motherhood and do it soon, our nation is headed for destruction.

The biggest battle we fight in life is the one we fight with ourselves. The issues we experience can either make us better or worse.

No matter where the issues come from, they can cause us to doubt ourselves. They can leave us with a lowered sense of self worth. When this happens, we become distrustful of ourselves and others. Our interactions with everyone, including our children, suffers.

Believing God has forsaken us; the emptiness we feel is often masked by quick fixes like drugs, alcohol, and sex. When it's all said and done, we're still empty.

It is important we take the time to relieve ourselves of the guilt associated with falling for the mess that has become our lives. Second, we must find comfort in knowing God is Jehovah Shalom; the God of peace. He will give you a peace that surpasses all understanding. Finally, we must believe God will honor his word and be with us even until the end of the world.

I am at the end of my sermon as a minister of motherhood. The fruit of my labor is sweet and satisfying. My children are grown up and so am I. They are making successful lives for themselves independent of me. I, too, am learning to live a life independent of them. I am no longer their disciplinarian and protector. Instead, I am their mentor and friend. My time now belongs to me. I must admit, sometimes I don't really know what to do with my time. There aren't any basketball games to go to, no parent-teacher conferences to attend, and no field trips to chaperone. But, as usual, when one door closes, God opens another.

The Bible tells us; there is a time and a place for everything. Just as the seasons change, so do the times of our lives. This is my season; a season for new vision, new opportunities, and new direction.

Understanding that God turned what the devil meant for evil in my life into something good, I can now share the lessons that I learned. What are those lessons? Thank God for praying Mamas. My mother's prayers have carried me and my prayers carry my children. The prayers of the righteous availeth much. Never underestimate the power of prayer.

Your body is a temple. Don't give it away. Let God choose for you because when he does, I'm a witness that everything works out in the end. Developing common interests and taking time to get away for ourselves, has proven to

The Ministry of Motherhood

make our marriage stronger. Learning to listen and be heard, and being able to agree to disagree, opened new doors of communication for us. Developing a closer relationship with God enlightened us on how we could better minister to one another. Having a teachable spirit allowed both of us to work on ourselves. Without that, we would have ended long ago. My husband and I have been married for fifteen years.

Love your children. Really love them. Not with material things, but with your time, your effort, and yes, when necessary, with discipline. Let them know that you're always in their corner. Teach them love, compassion, and honesty. . Encourage them, be kind and understanding, listen to them, take time for them, take time with them, be interested in their interests, and show your unconditional love and approval. Know your strengths and weaknesses as a parent and ask God to provide you wisdom and knowledge in those areas where you are not strong. Seek wise counsel from other mothers around you. Don't expose them to public ridicule, don't set unrealistic goals, be willing to apologize, consider them in family decisions, and be tolerant and understanding. Participate in their school activities. Encourage their dreams. All things are possible with God

Most importantly, teach them the ways of the Lord. To God be the glory, neither of my sons has become a statistic. To the contrary, they are both college educated, well rounded young men who love the Lord and understand the meaning of giving back to the community.

As for me, well, to say that God has done exceedingly and abundantly more than I could ever ask would be an understatement. Authoring several books, hosting an internet radio show, and traveling the country speaking to women's groups about empowerment wasn't in my plan, but, I guess that's why the Bible says lean not to your own understanding.

Whenever I'm asked what I would say to a woman aspiring to be where I am, my response is this: "Don't aspire to be where I am, aspire to be where God wants you to be. Allow him to lead you according to His plan for your life. If it happens that you end up being an author or an educator, then so be it. Make sure God is in the mix. Open yourself to the possibilities and be ready to be blessed abundantly."

The Ministry of Motherhood and its subsequent outreach are efforts at becoming a catalyst for change in the lives of mothers and their children. The Ministry will live out the tenets of Titus 2 by teaching women good things, including how to love their children.

It is the hope of the author that mothers everywhere will claim the gift God has given them and become responsible for raising their children in the admonition of the Lord, regardless of their circumstances. Like Hagar, mothers must come out of the wilderness and help their children become the men and women God has called them to be. Mothers, minister to your children so that the sermon your life preaches leads to revelation.

PRAYER OF THANKSGIVING

Father in Heaven, I shout joyfully to You. I come before Your presence with thanksgiving; for You are a great God. You are my God and I am Your daughter. I give thanks to You Lord, for you are a good God. I enter into Your gates with thanksgiving and into Your courts with praise.

To You, O Lord, I lift up my soul, in You I trust, O my God. I thank you God that You have shown me Your ways and taught me your paths. Thank you God, for remembering me according to Your love and not for the sins of my youth and my rebellious ways. I thank You for Your favor. I confess that every good and perfect gift has come from You. I thank You for every person that You placed in my life, the good and the bad. I thank You that no weapon that was formed against me ever prospered, and I thank You that you did not give me the spirit of fear, but of love power and a sound mind.

I pray that Your will be done in the lives of mothers and their children. Harden not the heart of the fathers, and suffer them to do what is right by their children.

Father, forgive us for our sins of disobedience, selfishness, un-forgiveness, fornication, rebellion, and hatred. We will be quick to forgive those that have trespassed against us.

Lead us not into temptation, but deliver us from the evil one.

You alone are the one, true living God. Yours is the kingdom, and the power, and the glory, forever, Amen.

DISCUSSION QUESTIONS

How can you use your words to build up and encourage your children each day?

Who is the power behind your family?

What do people see when they look at your family?

What traits do you admire about other families?

How can you incorporate those traits into your family?

What positive aspects are being built into your own family?

How can your children be a blessing to you?

What does it mean for your children to be a gift from God?

How can you keep your desires for your child's life from overpowering God's desires for their life?

How can you guide your children into the acceptance of Christ and His plans for their lives?

How can you help your child nurture their talents?

How can you be a good role model for your child?

How can you help your child develop responsibility?

What are some ways you can show your children unconditional love?

ABOUT THE AUTHOR

Coming from a legacy of preachers, Cheryl Lacey Donovan is walking in her destiny. An anointed woman of God, her mission is to challenge you to look inside yourself for change, to identify the strongholds in your life, and to tear them down with the help of the creator. Once you have crossed her path, your life will never be the same. Cheryl Donovan is an acclaimed author, inspirational speaker, and compelling advocate for personal empowerment. Her book Women What the Hell are You Thinking remained in the top 10 of Amazons Hot New Releases during its first two months of publication. Her new work The Ministry of Motherhood is destined for the bestseller list as it ministers to mothers who are living through what Cheryl has already overcome. Cheryl believes in Psalms 11:25 which says, She who refreshes others will herself be refreshed; therefore, she tries to be transparent as she speaks and writes about her valley to mountain experiences. Cheryl's internet radio talk show Worth More than Rubies reaches thousands of listeners each Friday and has impacted women all across the nation. Her syndicated column of the same name can be found in both print and online magazines. She is also a regular contributor to several blogs including her own, "Worth More Than Rubies," with blogspot.com. Cheryl's work was most recently published in the anthology "The Triumph of My Soul." Cheryl has been recognized nationally for her work. She has been the featured author on radio talk shows such as Artist First, Power Talk FM, An Hour to Empower with Mo and Mickey, and Urban Echoes' Voices and Vibes. Her interviews have also appeared in Empowering African American Women Magazine, Swaggie's Blog Spot, AA Kulture Zone, The Book Suite, and Women's Self Esteem. She was recently awarded the 2007 Literary Power Award and she has been nominated in several categories for the Infini Awards. Cheryl will be featured for the inaugural season of What Shall We Read, a literary program which airs on CAN-TV in Chicago. She will also be inducted into the 2008 Who's Who in Black Houston. Visit the author online at www.CherylLaceyDonovan.com.

The Ministry of Motherhood
Ordering Information

Yes! Please send me _____ copies of Cheryl Lacey Donovan's, *The Ministry of Motherhood*.

Please include $15.00 plus $2.00 shipping/handling for the first book and $1.00 for each additional book.

Send my book(s) to:
Name:_____
Address:_____
City, State,
Zip:_____
Telephone:_____
Email:_____

Would you like to receive emails from Peace In The Storm Publishing?
____Yes   ____No

Peace In The Storm Publishing, LLC.
Attn: Book Orders
P.O. Box 1152
Pocono Summit, PA 18346
www.PeaceInTheStormPublishing.com

www.ingramcontent.com/pod-product-compliance
Lightning Source LLC
Chambersburg PA
CBHW051432290426
44109CB00016B/1521